Spit And Polish For Husbands

BRYAN DAVIS

Spit And Polish For Husbands

Becoming Your Wife's Knight in Shining Armor

BRYAN DAVIS

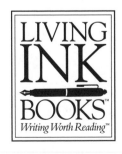

LIVING
INK
BOOKS
Writing Worth Reading™

Fairest Lady, I am your knight in shining armor. I raise my shield to protect your body, to guard your purity, and to defend your honor. I raise my sword to vanquish your enemies, to cut away your burdens so that I may take them as my own, and to point the way to the next horizon. I raise my voice to sing your praises in the streets, to shout the joy of being your husband, and to praise my Redeemer for the unspeakable blessing of awakening at your side at the dawning of each new day.

Contents

Acknowledgments

To my savior, Jesus Christ, the holy warrior-king who will come again, riding on a white horse to wage war in righteousness, the same humble servant who freely gave His life for my soul. Thank you for being the perfect knight in shining armor.

To my writing friends, thank you for your encouragement, especially Rosemary Upton, Kistler London, Elaine Colvin, Jean Dickman, Donna Tinsley, Billie Wilson, Tom Tacker, and Cecil Murphey. Your help, both at your desks with your editing pens and on your knees with your fervent prayers, will someday become jewels in your crowns.

To everyone at AMG Publishers, especially my editor, Dan Penwell, and to my agent, Steve Laube, thank you for your continued support and wise counsel.

Introduction
Who Is This Knight?

What is a "knight in shining armor"? Is he merely a symbol of romantic ideas, a young girl's fantasy? Is he just an impossible dream fashioned by long-suffering wives who despair that their husbands will never become what they had hoped?

No. This knight is not a dream or a storybook myth. He is embodied in every man who waits as his bride walks down a wedding aisle, every man who declares, "I do" in the presence of witnesses. He is neither fantasy nor fancy.

Is this knight a real man? Yes, he's as real as house repairs, electric bills, and stale coffee. He takes morning strolls, watches sports on television, and works on his car. And he's every bit as real as the woman who lovingly gazed into his eyes on a glorious wedding day. Look in the mirror and you'll see him.

Each of us can be that knight, the gentle warrior who walks in honor, humility, and truth. He is the man after God's own heart who doesn't stray when the sound of battle begins. Each of us has been given a guiding light, the Word of God, to teach us how to be the kingdom warrior who seeks the glory of his King.

When we first don our suits of armor, they glow with the glory of the King Himself, the fresh anointing grace that He bestows. As the years advance, however, our wedding anniversaries come and go, and our armor constantly needs attention. We are called to keep our armor shining brightly. We have to make sure that we never lose sight of our goal, glorifying God by the way we live our lives.

Husbands, in this book I will appeal to you as men. We feel in our spirits the upward call of God, the trumpet's signal to rise up and pursue God's kingdom with all the strength we can muster. As men, we have a perspective that females may not understand. We have passion that runs deeper than any outward emotion can express. We have a calling that awakens us in the early hours and echoes our names, beseeching us to answer a mysterious challenge to greatness.

My approach in this book combines a passionate call to our masculine hearts with a dose of humorous asides and anecdotes. You will understand that a call this serious will weigh too heavily without a bit of fun to lighten our load. We will not arrive at our goal by creating a huge guilt trip, so we might as well have a laugh along the way.

We must take care, however, not to ignore the entreaty. We are to be knights of the legendary Arthurian mold, not plastic Don Quixote figurines who blindly chase the windmills of our day, meaningless activities that take our time but have no lasting value. We are to be men of real principle, not salesmen who want to shine just for the sake of show. So when the going gets serious, we'll get dead serious. My bottom-line message is a solemn charge to every man of God who reads this book. When the laughing stops, we will strap on our swords and go to war.

Your Fair Maiden

Who can argue with the fact that a good woman stands behind every good man? She is more than a helpmate; she is the heart of passion, the inspiration behind the drawing of the knight's sword. It is said that a thousand ships launched for Helen of Troy. Should we be surprised that a woman can inspire each of us to greatness?

Your warrior heart is reflected in how you shine for your wife. In your youth and vigor, you probably radiated the passion of the courageous soldier for God. You possessed a heart of fire, eyes of steel, and singleness of purpose. Your spiritual vision was irresistible.

As we age, our vision must remain clear. Our shining armor must not be allowed to fade. We must continue to be for our wives the valiant knights who never lose our passion for God's kingdom. In turn, our wives will be godly women who nourish us, build us up, send us off to battle, prepare our beds for our return, and kneel at the altar until we come home to their arms. Without their support, none of us husband-knights could ever survive the rigors of our calling.

Rock and Jack

Let's take a quick look at one husband who's trying to keep his armor shining, but is having a hard time figuring out what he's doing wrong. We'll let him speak for himself.

The name's Rock Squarejaw, and I'm a knight. You know, the whole knight in shining armor thing. Right here's my horse, Starlight Confession. I named him that 'cause I thought it sounded kind of romantic, but now I just call him SC for short. He's a class act, a real charging steed. You should've seen us moving when I swept my wife-to-be off her feet. I saw her from a distance. Our eyes met, and they did that sparkly thing where both of us saw a gleam in each other's eyes. So I whispered to SC, "That's the girl for me," and the rest is history. I took her to my palace. She was really happy, at least for a while. Now it's been a few years, and she doesn't look at me the same way she used to. I don't see that sparkle in her eyes anymore. I'm the same guy I used to be, at least I think I am.

I have a friend named Jack, Jack Broadshoulders. He seems to get along great with his wife. She looks at him like he's a movie star or something, even though he's turning gray and his bald spot's so big it can be seen on satellite photos. The last time my wife looked at me like that, she had a fever of 104 degrees. I wonder if I'm doing something wrong.

Rock Squarejaw is our convenient straw man. There's probably no one on earth quite as dense as he is, but we'll use him for expediency. He's only a foil for my introduction, anyway, so I'll dispense with him in short order. Rock believes he's the same guy he used to be, at least he feels that way inside. He's not really aware of what his beloved maiden sees from her perspective. The shining armor that once attracted her has lost its sheen—the gleam in his character that made her take notice, the gleam that allowed her to deliver her most precious gift—trust in him. She gave herself to a man she really hardly knew. She trusted an image, but what Rock portrayed for her wasn't real.

Jack Broadshoulders, on the other hand, kept his gleam. His shining armor was a reflection of his true character, so his outer glow never changed. He wasn't just courting a mate, dangling a fishing lure on a line until he made his catch. Jack was just being himself, and it lasted through the years making his gray, balding head of no consequence to his wife's adoring eyes.

Our Charge as Knights

Whether we resemble a knight or a knave or someone in-between, it's up to us to keep our armor shining, to apply that spit and polish of masculine bravery and everyday courtesy, to be gentle warriors. Talking about spit sounds kind of gross, but we need to get our hands dirty if we want to earn the reputation of a clean conscience. From taking out fermenting garbage to changing the diaper on a volcanic baby, we men have to take a share of the nasty jobs. This sacrificial service is the spit that makes us shine. Sometimes it takes dirty deeds to kindle our wives' gleaming eyes.

We also have to follow our vision, the quest that God has given us. Women don't want boring television watchers who fossilize right before their eyes. They want men of courage who will take them along on the ride of their lives.

Husbands of valor and all husbands of valor wannabe's, take note. We are to live the great adventure—the noble quest of knighthood—to sweep our wives toward an exciting horizon, to live as the husbands God has called us to be.

Our call to duty begins in the mundane events of day-to-day life—in the bathroom, in the kitchen, and on our

xvi   SPIT AND POLISH FOR HUSBANDS

knees in prayer. Newspaper headlines won't spell out our faithfulness; the satisfied sighs of our godly wives and children will prove our success.

Let's not follow the popular prescriptions of the day. Let's not settle for mediocrity. We're not spineless men. We're men of God, empowered by His Spirit, dedicated to a holy vision.

Mount your steed, draw your sword, and follow me. Are you ready for the ride?

The Toilet and Other Female Domains
The Lid, the Paper, and Aiming to Please

The Character of the Knight:
Inner Beauty or Mere Plumage?

It is often said that a man is the ruler of his domain, the lord of his castle. But then again, many foolish things are often said.[1] A single man usually has no problem running the compartments of his home. The toilet seat can always stay up, laundry day is based on the underarm sniff test, and eating ravioli directly from the can is simply the most practical way to keep the kitchen clean.

When a man gets married, however, everything changes. The dominion is now shared sovereignty, a division of power with delegated authority, and how he handles that challenge requires skilled diplomacy. A man's ability to respectfully give

---

1. Warning. Blatant chauvinism will follow. I will flaunt old-fashioned stereotypes and archaic values. Even if such prehistoric views make you gag, please read on. I hope you'll find passages of deep respect for both genders and helpful hints that even ardent feminists will enjoy.

up portions of his realm requires a quality called selflessness,[2] a crucial part of a man's shining armor.

Selflessness is the key to all courtship rituals. It's the first gleam that a woman notices in her knight's shining armor. Few women are attracted to a guy who hands her a bag of his dirty socks and underwear during a first meeting, saying, "Don't use bleach; it gives me hives."

Proper courtship involves exposing an inner selfless character, and a knight's first act of sacrifice includes giving time and attention.[3] To that he may add the price of entertainment and food. He may include chivalrous acts, sacrifices of priority and convenience such as holding the door open or carrying heavy packages. In the spirit of a true gentleman he might even step into puddles or mud and carry her across to help her avoid sullying her clothes.

Think back to your courtship period. When you acted as a suitor for your bride-to-be, didn't you display kindnesses that reflected your dedication to meet her needs? These acts defined you as someone who is willing to make a sacrifice. You painted a picture of a man who cares, a man who'll take care of her.

Have you made that commitment last? Showing acts of sacrifice during courtship and then abandoning your wife after "catching the prize" is nothing more than a lie. It's a peacock showing off his exquisite plumage to impress a hen with a mere display of feathers. There's no real inner beauty to match.

Dying to self is the foundation of being a good husband; it's the dubbing of knighthood, our initiation into the profession of spiritual nobility. And the putting on of shining armor is the practice of self-sacrifice, expressed through day-to-day

---

2. Or in the case of those who haven't yet learned these lessons, it could be called, "I really need someone to clean my house."

3. Although a woman also shares in this sacrifice, I leave examination of her role for another book.

activities that display inner holiness. There are no substitutes, no shortcuts. Every tip in this book that helps us to shine our armor is based on our decisions to deny self. In contrast, every sin that we could possibly commit originates in selfishness.

If Christ hasn't made our hearts pure, and we're seeking an outward shine, we'll just be putting on a show to impress—strutting with peacock feathers. It may look pretty for a while, but it won't last. And it probably won't fool our wives for long. A mask wears out and a façade becomes transparent, but inner light, fired by the beauty of God's holy character, lasts forever.

Domain Theory—Peace at the Borders

Every husband has a domain. Whether he has an ocean of cattle on a thousand mountainous acres, or just an old Labrador retriever on thirty square feet of crabgrass, they're his, and his call to rule over them is undeniable. A man's wife, although she has submitted herself to her husband's authority, is not part of that domain. She's not an acre of land, a heifer in the herd, or a faithful dog. She's a partner, an overseer, someone who stands at his side to help him take care of what is now theirs together.

When a man gets married, he gives up autonomy; he allows his spouse to share his authority within his realm and transfers authoritative power to her. As time goes by, this imputed muscle is clearly demonstrated. His wife's instructions to their children should carry the same influence as his own. Her words to a laborer he has hired should crackle in the worker's ears like the commands of the lord of the house. She has the power to negotiate "foreign affairs"—scheduling activities with the outside world, making day-to-day purchases, and signing legal documents. She is more than an ambassador; she understands the heart of the ruling knight.

Whether these abilities come naturally to her or not, her husband's loving guidance will make his armor shine in her eyes. He has demonstrated a willingness to rely on her, giving up his position as sole and omnipotent ruler by delegating authority to his trusted mate. This is real authority that can't be taken back. It can be retrained, redirected, or refocused, but the authority is hers, exercised in humility as she stays in constant communication with her husband.

As we husbands apply this principle of shared authority in our homes, we must be careful to maintain balance. Delegation of authority doesn't mean relegating all authority to our wives in all areas; nor does it free us from noticing their activities. We are, in effect, guardians over their efforts.

Sometimes in your wife's dealings with the outside world, a person or a business will fail to treat her with due respect. People will not recognize her as an authority in your home, or they won't see your arm of power backing her up. Because she is a woman, some will try to use her weaker frame to their advantage, foolishly assuming that her only clout is the feminine physique they can see with their eyes. In cases such as these, you must step in with power to demonstrate to your wife your passionate commitment to back her authority. Your act of support will correct the foolishness of anyone who perceives outward vulnerability as a means of opportunity, treating the beloved extension of your authority as a powerless peasant.

A Woman's Place

Some female domains don't require our watchful eyes. In fact, some places are so sacred to the female world that it would be best if we view ourselves as visitors rather than sovereigns. The bathroom is such a place.

It's true that men use the bathroom, too. But that's the extent of it. It's a place to quickly wash, shave, relieve the pressures of six cups of morning coffee, and then desert. There are times when pausing to read a magazine might be in order, but only out of necessity. The bathroom is not our domain; we don't want to spend much time there.

A typical woman, on the other hand, views the bathroom as a natural place to dwell. It's an inspection station, a refuge for contemplation, and a hiding place in which to weep. Bathrooms in the homes of other people are a curiosity to her, a place to learn about the habits of friends and acquaintances. Even a public restroom can be a social hall, a place for women to convene and make plans for the evening.

The bathroom is also a woman's weigh station, a place to check out the ravages time has wrought. Don't we want our wives to look as attractive as they can? Of course we do. They know we like to look at them, so we might as well confess our admiration of their frame and form. It's natural for us to enjoy their physical beauty, so we shouldn't try to hide this God-given pleasure. If we show them respect and honor, loving them in word and deed, they'll respond by doing what they can to fight age and gravity.

When your wife primps and fusses, she's probably doing it for you. The time she spends in the bathroom is her way of returning the favor, a way to bring delight to your eyes. Yes, she looks just fine without all that fussing, and yes, some women are overly concerned with how they appear to the outside world. But a loving wife has eyes only for her husband.

When she shaves her legs, she thinks about how smooth they'll be against yours. When she pulls on a dress and scrutinizes it in the mirror, she pictures how the color will reflect in your eyes. When she scowls at the extra three pounds that the scale is obviously lying about, she'll wonder if you'll notice them when you take her in your arms.

Yes, the bathroom is a woman's domain, and it's for our own good that we learn to recognize that fact. The sooner we understand the mystery of Lavatory Land and the identity of the reigning mistress of that province, the sooner we'll learn how to keep our armor bright. The surest way to create tarnish is to usurp what is rightfully hers.

Now it's time to get perfectly practical,[4] and this next sentence may be the most important tip I give in the entire book: keep the toilet closed and clean.

The age-old stereotype is true. Women really do *hate* it when the toilet seat is left up. A gracious woman might not complain verbally, but don't let her silence fool you; she still hates it. Let's examine the reasons behind this attitude that seems overblown in the minds of most males.

First of all men, how would you like it if you had to sit down every time you went to the bathroom? Cold porcelain isn't a great way to awaken a bottom each and every chilly winter morning. What could be worse? Well, try sitting on cold porcelain that's been topped with drips of stale urine. How's that for stoking the fires of romance?

What kind of insensitive clod would not only forget to lift the lower seat, but also not bother to clean it after making a mess? A man might protest, "I was sleepy, and I wasn't thinking." Is that a good excuse? Of course not! If we really love our wives, we'll think about their needs before our own need for sleep. We'll be so in tune with protecting them that our first thoughts will be for their comfort. It's easy to lift the seat. It's even easier to lower it when we're done. And if we do splash, at the very least we can snap off a few pieces of toilet paper and clean it up.

---

4. You'll learn as the book goes on that I love alliteration.

Is that such a hard chore to do for our soul mates, the love of our lives?

If you've already messed up in this area, the next time it's really cold outside, get up early and put a space heater near the toilet. Turn it up high, and let it radiate all over that chilly porcelain. What a great way to make her feel warm all over! It's a great way to say, "I'm sorry."

Practically speaking, leaving both lids down just makes good sense. It keeps a toilet's natural fragrance from permeating the room. It keeps the cat from drinking from its tasty reservoir.[5] And leaving the cover down can discourage two-year-olds from playing boats with whatever plastic toy they bring into Lavatory Land. A closed lid also makes a handy place to sit while putting on shoes before leaving the bathroom.

Now I move on to the toilet paper, which I will call by its popular name, TP. Men see TP as a utilitarian device, the use of which is obvious. It doesn't matter if it's white, pink, or of floral design; it all gets flushed anyway. Women, however, tend to view TP as a symbol, a sign of the care with which they arrange their domain. Yes, the TP gets flushed, but everyone has to use it first so it might as well be pretty and smell nice. And finally, it must always come off the roll in the proper direction.

What *is* the proper direction? Through the years, I've heard a dozen strident arguments for each side, from the "over-the-top" gang and the "from-underneath" defenders. After studying the tissue issue in great depth, I've discovered a concrete solution, an undeniable truth. There really is a correct way against which there can be no argument. The correct way is the way your wife wants it to be.

---

5. I say "tasty," although I've never tried it. Cats, however, seem to think it's the nectar of the gods.

If the toilet paper is nearly empty, carefully note which way the paper leaves the roll. Does it come over the top when you pull it, or does it roll out from underneath? Next, go ahead and use the rest of it. Don't be shy; the environmentalists will never know. Slip off the cardboard tube,[6] and put a new TP roll in place. If the tissue doesn't come off the roll the same way it did before, take it off, turn it around, and reattach it. It should then be correct.

The point I'm making is simple. When issues arise that are of trivial importance to men, we should willingly do the little things that make our women happy. It should bring us a measure of joy every time we lean over to properly place the lids and paper, to clean the sink after shaving, and to wipe down the glass door or vinyl curtain after showering. We, who are to be like Christ is to the church, should be willing to die for our wives. Why should we even give a second's delay to doing something so easy and trivial as moving a lid or placing a roll of TP on the holder correctly? What does a lid or roll of TP weigh? Not much. Our little sacrifices, especially in our women's domains, bring far more joy to them than we can imagine.

Porcelain Prodding

If you don't believe that your minuscule moments of kindness will make your wife rejoice, put it to the test. Without being asked and without mentioning it after the fact, scrub out the sink or wash the mirror. Don't worry. She will notice. And if she asks you why you did it, don't say,

---

6. We save our cardboard tubes for our gerbils. It's a natural way to recycle. I just thought I'd add that in case an environmentalist is reading this.

"Cause it was dirty," or "It looked like it needed it." That will make her think you're upset with her housekeeping. Instead, just shrug your shoulders and say, "I made a mess," or "Just doing my part to help out."

Since the bathroom is a place you visit multiple times a day, it provides many opportunities to shine your armor. I'll list a few more, and once you see the pattern of service and self-sacrifice you'll be able to come up with some of your own.

1. A Snappy Towel
   After you take a shower, put a clean towel on the rod for her,[7] keeping it neatly creased and looking fresh. A crisp, clean towel says "I'm thinking about you" without ever making a sound, and silent expressions are always more profound than the most romantic sonnets.
2. Aim to Please
   Put a sign on the wall above the toilet that says:

FIVE STEPS TO A HAPPY MARRIAGE

Step 1 — Lift seats
Step 2 — Urinate (Aim with accuracy)
Step 3 — Clean up any splashes
Step 4 — Flush
Step 5 — Lower seats quietly

Just posting these instructions will help her know that you're really going to make an effort as you aim to please.

---

7. I'm assuming there's not already a usable towel on the rod. We don't want to add to the pile of laundry.

3. Socks and Jocks
   Pick up your dirty clothes and put them into the
   laundry hamper or wherever your family stores them
   until laundry day arrives. Hang your wet or sweaty
   ones up to dry, remembering to deposit them in the
   laundry stash later. Nothing says "I don't care about
   your feelings" like dirty underwear in the middle of
   the floor or stinky, wet socks on the vanity. A message of apathy darkens her heart as surely as the rising odor offends her nostrils.

Matters Small and Great

As we give of ourselves in trivial matters, our actions will
prove our commitment to sacrifice in larger ones. As
Jesus said, "He who is faithful in a very little thing is faithful
also in much; and he who is unrighteous in a very little thing
is unrighteous also in much" (Luke 16:10). Our attention to
detail will prove the validity of our marriage covenant. When
we're faithful in meeting our wives' needs in small matters,
they'll trust us in greater ones. On the other hand, if we're
unwilling to be servants in something so small as lifting or
closing a toilet seat, how can our wives trust us when greater
trials come along? We might say, "Of course I'll be there for
the big stuff," and so we might, but verbal promises are not
what solidifies their faith in us. It's the little, day-to-day acts
of servanthood that prove our commitment.

Other Domains—The Kitchen

Another female domain is the kitchen. Yes, I know
some men are great cooks, and some women can't

even burn coffee right, but that's not the point. God gave every woman certain gifts, and one of them is a motherly desire to meet the needs of her family, including nutritional requirements.

When it comes to cooking, a man usually invades the kitchen in order to create a masterpiece, taking pride in the charisma of heavenly scents in willing nostrils, the bliss of a tangy new sauce rippling over taste buds, or the beauty of blended colors that spangle in guests' eyes as his magnum opus is presented at the table.[8] Who cares if it's nutritious? It's a sensual tour de force!

Don't get me wrong. A husband should cook now and then. It's part of his nature to create, whether he builds with wood and nails, brick and mortar, or lasagna noodles and tomato sauce. Creative energy needs an outlet, and an occasional kitchen invasion can alleviate a lot of his pent-up pressure.

A woman, on the other hand, views the kitchen as a place of sustenance, a storehouse of basic essentials. It's where vitamins and minerals answer to roll call in a hurried assembly of the two-and-a-half basic food groups—bread, meat, and pasteurized, processed cheese food. Since the children had their chewable vitamins this morning, if the midday collection has iron, calcium, and at least two major vitamins, it'll do just fine for lunch.[9] A parade of colors and fragrant aromas might be nice, and she'll strive toward that goal, but if it's nutritious and tastes good enough to keep the kids from saying, "Yuk," she'll ring the dinner bell.

---

8. Yes, I know this description is overdone. That's the point.

9. Official disclaimer: my wife does an awesome, tireless job of selecting nutritious foods for our meals. We don't always eat it, but she makes sure we are supplied with every necessary nutrient.

Although she might want to create something special on occasion, a wife's mission is really a thrice-daily quest to keep her husband and children from getting scurvy. As a mother, she feels called to this duty, so give her all the honor due her great commission. Her job can be torturous, so don't make it any worse.

In my house, if ungrateful tongues reject my wife's latest attempt at proper dietary provision, I know mine better not be one of them. Even if the meal really is one huge "Yuk," I eat it with a smile on my face. Taking a bite of a live grub-worm would be more palatable to me than risking the slightest chance of disappointing my long-suffering wife.

Stovetop Tips

We should always treat the kitchen as a woman's domain; it's one of her workplaces. It's not a place of refuge, like the bathroom, but it's still a province that should be completely in her power. If we do cook on occasion (and we should), we must clean up our messes thoroughly. If we leave our wives with a hundred pots and pans to scrub, we haven't removed any loads from their shoulders.

Even if we don't cook, we should do the dishwashing or arrange for our older children to do it. If no children are available, cleaning up dinnertime messes is a good job for a husband and wife to do together. It provides a short time to talk, to catch up on the day's activities.

Here's your first tip. I find that clearing the table and putting away leftovers is a good task for me. The hunt for the right-sized plastic dish and matching lid is an adventure, almost like a safari, and it helps me turn out a decent lunch for myself the next day. I can keep track of where everything is, and I don't have to launch a refrigerator scavenger hunt when I'm in a hurry.

In my experience, searching through refrigerator leftovers is a man's assignment. When six or seven unlabeled margarine containers stare me down, opening each one to discover its contents can be dangerous. One smells like old socks, but it looks like stiff gravy with a bad toupee. When I touch the second, it growls and snaps shut. Nope. That one needs to cool off a little more. The third margarine container holds, well, margarine. Now that's strange. The fourth smells okay and has no growl and no hair. Lunch!

This brings me to the *second tip*. Men, if our wives don't take great joy in making our lunches for us, we should make them ourselves. This is one image of nostalgia that needs to be destroyed: the neatly packed cooler or brown bag sitting on the table just before we leave for work. We must not demand such a luxury. It places an unnecessary burden on our overworked wives, and we're perfectly capable of doing this task ourselves. It doesn't take much effort to slap a piece of meat and lettuce on a sandwich bun, grab an apple, and slip an Oreo® or two into a bag.

When we get into the habit of making our own lunches, we open the door of opportunity for our godly wives to beat us to the punch if they have a spare minute or two. And, who knows, they might even slip love notes in with the cookies. Who says the cream in the middle is the best part? I look forward to the sugar I'll get at the end of the day.

Tip number three: When your wife is out of the house for an hour or two, give the kitchen a good cleaning. Sweep and mop the floor, wash and put away dishes, and wipe down all the counter surfaces after clearing the piles of stuff that have accumulated there.

My wife and I tend to stack the day's mail on the kitchen counter, and after several particularly busy weeks the "stuff-to-go-through-later" pile can become a foreboding mountain of doom. It takes a few minutes, but I can usually throw away about two-thirds of the stack, and we take care of the rest together when she gets home.

This tip can lead to a pretty big job, but even if you're not very good at cleanup duty, the kitchen will probably look better as a result of your efforts. Trust me, your wife will think it looks great, even if she doesn't say so right away.

Domain Theory — A Final Word

Men, we must take care to respect our wives' domains. It's worth it. From the bathroom to the kitchen, let's do the little things that fill their hearts with trust. In addition, let's be sure to keep our own domains in shape. The working world, the garage, and the world of tools and handiwork all need our care and commitment.

In any situation where conversation on equal footing or negotiation with a man must take place, it's up to us to be our families' mouthpieces if a conflict arises. We must never allow our wives to be in a position of trading intense words with a man; a woman should not be forced to verbally wrestle with someone physically stronger than she. Enforced authority outside the home is to be our domain.

Even when our wives come to the place of sharing our authority, we will be wise not to forget one of our most important duties—to protect them during difficult circumstances. Step in and take over when the world gets too pushy or becomes threatening. Knights, this is your domain. When you take control of difficult situations in your realms, your armor will shine like a beacon.

There are times when I have to make phone calls to the school superintendent to straighten out graduation requirements, or talk to the bank manager to delete a service charge on our checking account, or drive to the plumber's storefront when my wife discovers that the "fixed" pipes still leak. Some people are not willing to do what's right, and my wife's influence isn't always enough to persuade them. It's then up to me to exert my influence directly.

I could relate dozens of experiences in which my wife was unable to get a refund from a rules-oriented store clerk or was stymied by a red-tape specialist in the government. It seems that a firm, under-control male voice often lubricates rusty gears far better than a female's. Call it unfair; call it sexist. I call it a fact.

All of this attention to our wives' needs isn't coddling; it's the natural outpouring of our servant hearts, hearts made pure by the sacrifice of Christ, hearts molded into tenderness by His example in life and on the cross. Yes, my wife would survive without my acts of servanthood. If I were less of a servant, she would still clean my messes in Lavatory Land, strive to make nutritious meals for our family, and even pack my lunch and put it by the door. The only missing item would be the one I cherish most, the heartfelt love note nestled against the Oreos®, the sweet treat of love that gleams in her eyes. Losing that would be a tragedy.

Knowing my wife's deep passion for loving obedience to God, I believe she would do it all without a murmur of complaint. She also made a covenant, a commitment to meet my needs, just as I agreed to meet hers. If I were to shirk my commitments, however, she would be unable to prevent her spiritual eyes from seeing me as the lazy bum I would be. There would be no sheen in my armor, only the torn rags of a sniveling coward.

Remember, being a servant doesn't make a man into a doormat; it transforms him into a prince or even a king in the eyes of his appreciative wife. Any testosterone-laced fool can be a despot, treating his wife like the crud between his toes. It takes a heroic man—a knight in shining armor—to treat his wife with respect and compassion.

2

The Secret Cactus Code
Deciphering Her Words and Moods

The Great Communications Divide

Like most men, you probably respond to obvious signs of danger: the smell of smoke, a soaring flare, a terrified scream, or the quiet "uh-oh" of a toddler. But when it comes to helping your wife deal with her problems, your level of success depends on your ability to understand less-obvious distress signals and to interpret her special code language. You have to learn to cross the great communications divide.

Without question your wife is safe and secure in your home, right? Not exactly. Trust me, guys, home is no place to drop your shield. Every woman's life is filled with dragons, sorcerers, and spiritual pitfalls that threaten her mind and soul. It's up to you to be ready to defend her at the cost of your time, your pleasures, or even your life.

Part of your role is to ensure her comfort and safety as she lives out her role as your devoted wife and helpmate. When you pursued your wife-to-be, you probably brandished a shield of safety, drawing your sword when necessary to defend her body, spirit, and honor. This crucial aspect of your shining armor—a display of love—drew her into your protective arms.

The secret to success lies in knowing where her troubles are and in deciphering what her problems might be. When her moods change, she may suddenly seem to be under a sorcerer's spell. Most of the time she communicates normally, but all at once she begins to speak a foreign language, a form of communication that includes mind and body as well as speech, or lack thereof. We'll study how this type of dialogue affects her communication by observing the following vignette.

The scene is the bedroom,[1] a place of refuge many women seek when trouble visits. A woman sits on the side of the bed, her hands over her face. She's crying. Our hero, Husband Man, walks in.

"What's wrong?" Husband Man asks.

"Nothing," she replies, whimpering.

"Nothing?" Husband Man repeats, surprised. "Then why are you crying?"

The woman gives no reply. She just cries harder.

Husband Man, truly perplexed, sits by her side and reaches his hand toward her back, ready to comfort her. He's confused. *Should I speak? Should I sit quietly? What will my gentle touch communicate? Tenderness? Patience? A request for sex?*

---

1. Here is a fundamental point, men. When your wife's upset and she runs to the bathroom instead of the bedroom, she doesn't want to talk to you at all; she just wants to be alone. That's her domain. Stay out of it. The bedroom, however, is a place of invitation, a place of comfort and intimacy. If she goes to the bedroom, she wants you to come and talk.

He jerks his hand back. He doesn't want her to think it's for sex!

Time out! Okay, guys, let's give Husband Man plenty of time to consider his options. In the meantime, think about what you would do. Has this ever happened with your wife? Have you ever wondered why your wife won't just come right out and tell you what's wrong? Men usually want swift answers, machine-gun responses that get right to the point.

What if Husband Man says, "I'm here to provide the solution. Just tell me the problem, and be quick about it."

Oops, wrong choice. A husband should never, ever tell his wife to "be quick" about sharing a problem she's facing. What's the result if he does? Well, have you ever tried to tap syrup from a maple tree in January? "Be quick about it" freezes her spirit and causes her to tightly clench her teeth. Crowbars and chainsaws won't get her to speak if you stupidly blunder into the halls of impatience.

So what should Husband Man do to melt the icicles and loosen her communication latches? Dozens of books have been written about this basic difference between men and women and how they handle a crisis. Some authors claim that men and women are like aliens from other planets. That "Venus and Mars" gimmick made one author a fortune, but it seems that men and women are still millions of miles apart.

Although men and women are often like different species, the two genders are designed to be one flesh. When melded together in mind and spirit, man and woman can communicate on levels far deeper than any single gender can imagine. The problem is, no one has provided a sure way for the two genders to understand each other when a crisis interrupts life. There has been no recipe, no step-by-step instruction manual for men—until now, at least. (Obviously we should be charging much more for this book.)

So how can Husband Man understand the mind and emotions of his wife, grasping the deep mysteries that have eluded the Y chromosome ever since the first male chauvinist dragged a woman home by her hair? This information should come in a neatly wrapped box and be given to every male of our species the first time he develops any kind of relationship with a female.

Learning a Foreign Language

I remember when I first checked into my dorm room at college. The people who ran the dorm obviously had a glimmer of wisdom. They gave each new freshman guy a package filled with goodies that he would need: a bar of deodorant soap (Thank goodness!), small bottles of shampoo and conditioner, a miniature box of laundry detergent, and grocery coupons for Hamburger Helper. (Thank goodness, again!) What a great idea! A freshman guy's package of preparation, but there was nothing in the package about understanding women.

Through the centuries, men's preparation for life with women has been missing a crucial element, a way to understand their psyche. A pocket translator of women's speech and actions, a decoder ring of sorts that could listen to what women say and do and then translate it into Manspeak, should have been included in my freshman package. Their language conveys feelings using body language, facial nuances, and intonations of speech. To be sure, some women are fluent in Manspeak; they have learned to communicate on our plane of existence. Even these women, however, can revert to their native tongue during a time of crisis.

As knights who want to keep our armor bright, it's up to us to become experts in understanding the female language, a linguistic nightmare for men that we will call *Gunese* (pronounced goo-neeze).[2] Learning Gunese is a valiant quest. One of the most difficult dialects to master, it comes in many forms, sometimes seeming to contradict itself from one moment to the next. It's a language of beauty, complexity, and hair-pulling frustration. Gunese is not, however, a language we should (or could) learn to speak. Not only would we look like morons if we tried, our wives would think we're making fun of them.

Our duty is not to speak Gunese, but to convert it into something the masculine ear and mind can understand. God, in His wisdom, has only gifted women with this beautiful and powerful form of communication. Although we are to honor this language, we are not, under any circumstances, to reveal its name to our wives. The term Gunese must remain a secret among men. We certainly don't want women to hear us attaching a word that sounds like "goony" to the way they communicate. The results could be disastrous.

Before I continue my lecture on the complexities of the female language, please note that I'm teaching a generic dialect. There are many forms of Gunese, which vary based on age, culture, geographic regions, phase of the moon, day of their menstrual cycle, how much laundry is piled up, and current dietary restrictions. If, after reading these lessons, you still can't understand your wife, you're either linguistically challenged or one or more of the variability factors skews her brand of Gunese.

---

2. A weird name, yes, but all the cool names were taken. It's from the Greek word for woman, so it appears profound and deeply theological.

Although I'm nearly fluent in my wife's dialect, I can't guarantee that your wife's variation is compatible. If your wife is postmenopausal, lives somewhere north of the 29th parallel, and doesn't get enough fiber in her diet, she probably has a dialect foreign to the one I'm trying to teach. Every woman has a somewhat unique way of communicating Gunese, and her special voice is beautiful to behold and a necessary part of her being. If you glean the basics of Gunese and apply them well enough to interpret at least a few words of your wife's dialect, her love for you will know no bounds. You'll be more exciting to her than having three professional maids and a key to the Hershey's® warehouse. In short, your armor will sparkle.

Your first lesson involves your wife's decision to speak versus not to speak. If she tells you her problem directly, it's not necessarily a good sign. You see, a woman is verbally straightforward if her concern is simple and only minimally disturbing. The same is true, however, if Armageddon has begun. If she chooses to speak Manspeak, you can bet that her concern lies at one extreme or the other. If the faucet leaks, your wife will tell you about it point-blank. Simple problem, simple solution. On the other hand, if little Johnny sold his kid sister to nomadic gypsies or it's raining ten-foot-tall, fire-breathing ostriches outside, she'll probably tell you about that, too.

Anything in between, however, might be another story. If you happen to forget an important date, like her birthday or the day you first gave her a box of chocolates, a crisis of the heart arises, an emotional issue that bruises her soul. This crisis might not be revealed in distinct words. If she tried to relate the pain verbally, she may feel she couldn't do it justice. If she tried to use words to describe her feelings and spiritual ache, would she communicate a lie because her words would be inadequate? Would she sound silly to you because her concern is so trivial? Would you misinterpret her words and callously place her problem in a category you understand in order to apply a quick solution, an answer that couldn't possibly address her deeply felt need?

The most probable reason, however, is that the crisis that has set her heart to mourning seems insignificant in her mind, too, so she's embarrassed to tell you. She feels that something more is wrong, and she simply doesn't know what it is. Something has wrung her out like an old mop. It couldn't be the picky little problem she perceives, but it's the only one on which she can put her finger, making her unwilling to appear childish, petty, or fragile in the eyes of her beloved husband.

The Curse That Divides

When God toppled the Tower of Babel and confused the people's languages, He did so to make sure they wouldn't be able to communicate or cooperate in their prideful schemes. But this wasn't the first time God decreed such a division. When He cursed mankind in the Garden of Eden, He created a new distinction between man and woman, saying to Eve, "Your desire shall be for your husband, and he shall rule over you" (Gen. 3:16). God created a division between the genders that included giving them different languages, both in speech and in nonverbal interchange.

A wife, for example, desires to meld with the heart and soul of her husband, so she expresses herself spiritually, using a multitude of communication avenues. Words cannot express either the depth or the breadth of her feelings, so she can't always resort to the base inadequacies of Manspeak. Such a lowly appeal would dishonor her feelings; it would injure her spiritual integrity.

A man, on the other hand, is a monarch[3] of sorts. He communicates using precise, commanding words. If it's cold in the house, he'll state, "It's cold in the house!" or something equally profound. In contrast, a woman uses more subtle techniques, preferring body language and emotional draw. She'll rub her hands on her arms and shiver, maybe pushing her shoulder into her husband's ribs to get him to put his arm around her. When he does, he'll ask, like an Albert Einstein Pez® dispenser, "Are you cold?" To which she'll reply, "Not anymore." And when he processes this collection of verbal and nonverbal cues, he comes up with the "Manspeak" interpretation, "It's cold in here!" And rather than shout out, "Well, why didn't you say so?" he, like a good knight, runs to adjust the thermostat or get a sweater for her from the closet.

This difference in languages, as we've noted before, is well documented in other works. But we husbands have a unique goal for communicating with our wives. We're striving to maintain or revive the attraction that set their hearts on fire, to stoke or rekindle flames that roared when they agreed to join us at the end of the wedding aisle.

What brought about that dazzle, the spark that ignited your wife's fire? Simple. You spoke her language. Or, at least she thought you were trying to speak her language. Did you gaze into her eyes? In her language, you were saying, "I appreciate your inner beauty." Did you gently caress her hand? In Gunese you communicated a tender heart and your appreciation of nonsexual togetherness. Did you hold the door open for her? Whether you realized it or not, you were saying, "You're a lady of value, a treasure worth pampering." Although you weren't really speaking Gunese, for the

---

3. No, not the butterfly. A man is a ruler. No, not a measuring device. He's a sovereign. No, not the coin. Forget it!

moment you stumbled into her wavelength. You were being romantic, and that's the favorite channel of communication for almost every woman.

A villain uses these gestures merely as courting maneuvers in order to win a woman's heart for his selfish purposes. And once he captures her heart, he puts it away in a box, letting it throb in its prison, kept safely under lock and key. He has his hunted prey in the bag. Now he doesn't have to do all that touchy-feely stuff.

Pardon me while I deal with this wretch of a man. Fiend! Scoundrel! You played a game of deception, a traitor's ploy. She opened her heart and let it bleed, and for a time you collected every drop and cared for it as your own. Yet, now that she has given her heart to you, it bleeds into callous hands and you dash her weeping soul against the rocks. Away with you, you cowardly beast!

My fellow knights, if we were to follow this course, we would be villains, merciless cowards. What greater suffering can a woman experience than the loss of her soul mate, the man to whom she willingly gave her virgin heart, only to discover he had merely baited her and thrown her to the gutter like a one-night stand, a passing harlot in the night?

Fortunately most of us are not so devious. Our inability to understand our wives is more often due to a case of confusion rather than deception, coupled with weariness as we struggle to make translating Gunese a priority. As true knights, we need to remember our courting overtures and continue to reflect the value we perceive in our wives. Of course it's hard sometimes to draw out their feelings, but that's what self-sacrifice is all about. We must make the effort. Aren't they worth at least that, and so much more?

How do you do it? How do you take her hand and dance the intricate steps of love's communication waltz? You become a student of her body language—the way she sets her shoulders when she's sad, the angle of her brow when someone disappoints her, the thinness of her lips when she learns bad news. Are her hands on her hips, across her chest, or hanging limply at her side? How does her countenance change when you speak? As you learn every twitch of an eyebrow, every lovely line in her face, you'll understand her moods better and become a cryptologist of sorts who can identify shifts in her feminine mystique.

Although every woman has her own dialect, there are a number of universal cues that reveal a crisis. Crying, of course, is a giveaway. Silence when she's normally talkative is another. Although asking "What's the matter, Honey?" may sound trite and overused, it's the type of phrase you need to express in order to begin the sometimes tedious dance of male-to-female communication. She expects it, and any negative reaction to your question isn't due to the question itself; it's due to the crisis she's harboring in her heart. And please, don't forget to add the "Honey" or whatever your favorite TOE[4] might be. So, step one is simply to ask the question your wife is waiting for.

The Redemption That Unites

Let's go back to Husband Man as he tries to translate his wife's Gunese and respond it to effectively. He places his hand on her back and asks softly, "What's the matter, Honey?" If she pulls away from his touch, she is speaking the Gunese phrase for "You're part of my problem, so you'd better go away for a while." And so he should, probably feeling

---

4. Term Of Endearment. Since we all have ten TOES on our feet, we should have at least ten TOE's for our wives. Why? Just to make my hypothesis seem academically and scientifically sound.

as insensitive as a pot of potatoes. Husband Man, however, is not so unlucky. His wife merely says, "Oh . . . nothing." At this point, some husbands would get up and say, "Oh good. I'm glad it's nothing," and march happily out of the room whistling "Are You Ready for Some Football?" These dolts conveniently forget about the tears. Although women often cry for what we consider paltry reasons, they never cry for no reason at all. Husband Man is no pot of potatoes. He makes this trite but appropriate statement: "There must be something wrong, Sweetheart (a classic TOE). It's not like you to cry for no reason."

Husband Man[5] scores big this time. Not only has he correctly identified that a problem exists, he has paid his wife a compliment. He has petitioned her reason by appealing to her heart, the natural highway on which many women travel and travail. If he had said, "There must be something wrong, Sweetheart, because only an idiot would cry for no reason," not only would he be implying that she's an idiot, he would have shown himself to be a hypocrite by calling her Sweetheart one second and an idiot the next. (That's called stubbing your big TOE.)

Pleased with HM's soft words and the gentle backrub, HM's wife sighs. "Well, it's nothing I should be crying about, anyway." At this point she looks up into HM's eyes, a sure sign that HM has connected to her Gunese frequency. "It's just that my cactus died this morning, and it was a present from your mother. I was hoping she would be happy that I put it in the front yard where everyone could see it."

What runs through HM's mind now? *Is that all? Oh, come on! I'll go out and buy three cactuses if you'll just stop your blubbering!* If that's what he's thinking, he'd better not

---

5. I'm going to call Husband Man "HM" for a while, just for fun, and because I love acronyms.

say it or he'll cut off his Gunese connection faster than a flock of diarrhetic pigeons can paint his freshly washed car. HM is a more sensitive soul. Yes, he knows a cactus is just a plant, but he also realizes that his dear wife has invested her feelings in it, making it infinitely more valuable in her eyes, and therefore in his as well. He treasures her heart, knowing that if she has placed just one minuscule gram of her emotions into that plant, it has transformed into something more valuable than a collection of prickles and pears. Because of her emotional investment, that thorny bush was just one notch below "family," and HM is already planning a proper funeral because of its untimely demise.

HM knows from experience that something deeper lies behind his wife's sad face. Rarely would the death of a plant bring such sorrow. *Could it be*, he wonders, *that she's worried about her relationship with my mother, who might be distraught at the death of her gift?* How can HM learn the real cause of his wife's turmoil, a root of distress even she can't identify?

Remember the words God spoke after Adam and Eve sinned? A woman *desires* that her husband search for the real source of her troubles, because he is to watch over her soul, to *rule* over anything that scalds her emotions. He is to be her knight in shining armor. He is to search out and destroy any offending agent, or counteract any influence that threatens her spiritual well-being.

Don't forget; HM doesn't speak Gunese. He shouldn't cry, or even sigh. That's not his place. He's the defender of his wife's heart. It's time for him to draw his sword.

"Oh, no!" HM replies, "Not the cactus!" He thrusts his hand into his pocket and digs for his car keys, whether they're there or not. "I'm going straight to the nursery and give them a piece of my mind. How dare they sell my mother a faulty plant!" Like a dashing knight, HM is ready to defend his wife's honor. Of course the death of the plant wasn't his wife's fault; she's much too talented and dedicated.

The wife, half-pleased and half-amused, places a hand on his arm. "No, Babe. (Yes! A TOE from his wife. The Gunese connection is complete.) It was my fault. Really! I've been so busy with the kids' project books for school, I never watered the cactus after I planted it. I thought a cactus wouldn't need it."

Now HM understands the crux of the issue. *It's not the plant she's worried about; she's really stressed-out over the project books and her hectic schedule. She has put so much time into those workbooks, sitting up long hours with the kids, choosing and cutting out photos from wildlife magazines and correcting their clumsy prose.*

Now HM knows exactly what to do. "Give me the project book that has the most pages left to finish," he says boldly (and with a bit of well-disguised fear), "and I'll work with whoever[6] it belongs to. Then if there are still projects to be done, I'll pitch in on those, too."

She throws her arms around his neck. "Are you sure you have time?"

"I'm sure," he had better respond.

HM has done his work. He has delved into his wife's heart, translating each Gunese phrase along the way, and discovered what was at the root of her problem. As is the role of all husbands, he stood ready to provide a solution, but not until he connected with her on the Gunese wavelength. He searched out the enemy and vanquished it with a thrust of his sacrificial sword, giving of his time in order to set his imprisoned wife free.

---

6. Yes, I know he should have said, "whomever," and he dangles a preposition. HM is a great guy, but grammar isn't his gig.

Now they walk out of the bedroom, hand in hand, and she smiles and says, "How'd you like to go for a walk in the flower garden?" Ah! She's over the untimely death of the cactus. HM knows that her heart has been healed. He has cared for it with loving hands by communicating with her in Gunese. Although he extended his knightly service in unselfish compassion, expecting no rewards, the benefits of love have come back to him along with the restored mind and soul of his lovely bride.

If a husband seeks to understand his wife, as HM did in this example, her language actually brings them closer together. It unites them in mind and spirit. They aren't two soldiers in a foxhole counting enemy scalps or a pair of basketball players bumping chests in a testosterone-laced frenzy. They are a new species, a blend of masculine and feminine characteristics, a mysterious union, the image of Christ and His church. Didn't Christ make a sacrifice, taking the initiative to communicate with mankind, delving into our psyche by entering our plane of existence? You bet He did. Men, as the image of Christ in our marriage covenant, it's up to us to take the first step. We need to delve into our wives' conditions and understand their ways, remaining fully masculine as we explore the awesome wonders of the feminine nature.

A Practical Tip

Husbands, whether you're a freshman or a postgraduate student in the disciplines of marriage, here's the decoder ring to add to your package of helpful items, a summary of basic Gunese lessons. When your wife is faced with a problem, she'll let you know about it, but she may not use audible words. There are two likely reasons for this behavior.

1. She doesn't know what the real problem is herself.
2. She wants you to drag it out of her to show you really care.

Put a visible reminder in your bedroom. Get out a red crayon and a sheet of notebook paper, and scrawl the initials "PPP" in large, block letters. Tape the page to the wall next to the door. When your wife asks what it means (and she will), tell her it stands for "Perfect Patience Palace," the refuge where you'll do your best to exercise perfect patience when she's suffering. And then do it. Since this is a traditional place of sharing physical love, also make it your place of delving into her soul. If you see one of those telltale, body language cues that something's wrong, take her by the hand and lead her to the PPP, your place of Gunese translation. This will signal your readiness to communicate, your willingness to speak her language, and your sacrificialness[7] to purge her spirit of the troubles that would torment her mind.

Our efforts to communicate will go a long way, knights. As we demonstrate patience, compassion, and a generous dose of tenderness, we'll help our wives see our determination to envelop them in our protective arms, no matter what, even if it means learning the beautiful dialects of women.

We've made a good start here. Although we don't have a complete Gunese dictionary in hand, we do have a set of guidelines. When properly used, they'll allow any husband with intelligence greater than that of a cactus to translate his wife's unique dialect and respond with the sacrificial love that Christ showed to His beloved bride.

---

7. Okay, I ran out of "nesses," so I used a phony one. There's a phony "ness" in a loch in the highlands of Scotland, too, and books written about it have made a lot of money. That's a good enough precedent for me.

3

Slaying Dragons
Not Your Mother-in-Law

Dragons in Our Midst

Knights slay dragons. That's just what they do. It's a law of nature like dogs bark, computers crash before you can save your work, and crummy, federally mandated, water-saving toilets will clog every time well-metabolized teenagers use them.

If we want our armor to shine for our wives, we husband-knights need to take the laws of nature seriously. If we don't seek out and destroy the dragons in our world, our armor will be like a sheet of Reynolds Wrap®. Aluminum foil may look shiny, but it's as thin as a coward's worthless hide, and no wife feels safe in the arms of a tin soldier.

In keeping with the knights-in-shining-armor model, I'm going to use dragons to symbolize the evil influences in our current culture. The dragons of this world are the many and varied people and forces that attempt to attack the wives we love. Our goal is to recognize the presence of dragons and foil their plans.

Dragons of Authority

The telltale sign of dragons' evil influences always boils down to this: destructive activity disguised as innocuous or even friendly persuasion. A wife is particularly vulnerable to a dragon's advances. No, she's not necessarily gullible. With love overflowing from her heart, she's just more trusting than a suspicious member of the cynical male gender. She tries to find good in everyone.

We men know, without a doubt, that most men are power-hungry predators. No man in the world can be trusted without a thorough background check—no man except us, of course, and maybe Mr. Rogers.[1] Our caution, as long as it remains harnessed and reasonable, becomes our wives' shield of safety.

Dragons in our century, like the infamous dragon of old in the Garden of Eden, yearn to pull our precious wives toward destruction, using the most despicable tricks to lure them to the forbidden fruit[2] of this age. Whether it's vanity, materialism, social status, or extramarital sexual intimacy, dragons' fruit always comes in pretty packages, and their words of enticement slide off forked tongues on sonnets of silky charm. Remember, Eve was tempted by a noble goal, to be as wise as God. That's how a dragon works; he wraps his poison in a polished apple and presents it to a woman as a gift. It looks tasty, but if she takes a bite, she's no longer Snow White.[3]

If Adam had been present when Satan tempted Eve,[4] he would have chopped that slithering serpent into snakeburger

---

1. Now that Fred Rogers has passed away, he can most certainly be trusted. The great Captain Kangaroo has also died, another trustworthy man. But I often wondered about him. What was with that naval officer's outfit anyway? And how can a guy be so easily outfoxed by a couple of sock puppets?

2. Since the Bible used food to make its points, I will use food references, too. See how many you can find.

3. Rhyme intended.

4. I have heard theories that Adam actually was with Eve during her temptation, but I think the theories fail under close scrutiny.

meat. But Adam's sword and shield hung on the wall back home. This is a widely ignored fact. Adam's first mistake was not in eating the forbidden fruit; it was in allowing the dragon of his world to influence his wife. And look at the results—thousands of years of pain and suffering. Yes, when Eve returned with the fruit, Adam could have refused it, but he succumbed to the male gender's most alluring temptation, seduction by a woman who seeks a partner in her sinful condition. His wife became a temptress who took solace in misery's company, a Samson's Delilah who relished the power to make a great man stumble and fall.

Our wonderful wives are not like Delilah. Although they are responsible for their own actions, they could use a bit of our muscular prowess to help them win their personal battles. With sword and shield in hand, we can come to their aid, lending the hand they might need in order to conquer the serpent and crush his scaly head. Let's look at a few concrete examples of how modern-day dragon activity can bring danger to a wife.

In keeping with Satan's divide-and-conquer strategy, modern dragons look for opportunities to attack a woman when she's away from her husband. If she works outside the home, the enemy draws a bull's-eye target on her forehead. There are many ways in which dragons in the workplace can dangle forbidden fruit in front of a woman's eyes. The corporate dragon can offer position and prestige in exchange for her precious time: working longer hours, doing paperwork at home, or taking business trips with overnight stays. The supervisor dragon may dangle a larger paycheck if she'll just loosen up a little and wear a plunging neckline, sport a tighter skirt, or compromise her purity in other ways.

The ministry dragon is the most devious. He promises God's favor and spiritual fulfillment if she'll just teach one more children's class, run vacation Bible school for one more summer, or supervise the missionary society's bake sale in addition to her other volunteer ministries. This dragon mercilessly slurps her time away from her family, dangling a noble spiritual goal as a finely polished apple.

God, in His mercy, gave each husband a wife to be his helpmate. And what a sorely needed gift she is! A husband without his wife is like a cheeseburger without cheese or iced tea without ice. But if she physically separates herself from her man and goes to be the helpmate of another, her loyalties become divided. Being absent, he can't rise to defend his wife when a cunning dragon presents her with a compromising proposal.

I know a man whose wife climbed high in her profession as a nurse. She worked with a handsome and successful doctor—a wealthy man of influence. The poisoned apple of glamour and esteem lured her into the dragon's trap. She left her husband for the promise of personal prestige and ran off with the doctor like the proverbial dish with the spoon. The husband said, "What was I to do? How could I compete with that?"

Of course I felt bad for him. Certainly his wife bears the blame for her adultery, but his impotent attitude revealed a deeply rooted problem. He displayed little of the masculine sword of defense, preferring to throw up his hands in surrender. If he had been wary, he might have detected signs of divided loyalty and found the dragon lurking in the shadows. Where did she want to spend her time? What did she like to talk about? For whom did she dress up? The husband might have been able to rescue her before she allowed her heart to be captured. Perhaps a virile, vigilant knight could have averted this tragedy. A man who fears his inadequacy will soon find his armor becoming rusty and dull, and his wife may seek other avenues of fulfillment.

I'm not saying that a wife should always stay home, bare-foot and pregnant.[5] She should, however, answer to no one but her husband, leaving no room for a possible division of loyalty. If finances are so tight that more money is desperately needed, a husband treads dangerous ground if he chooses to send his wife out to collect an extra paycheck rather than working a second or third job himself to bring home the bacon. Her departure from the home should be a last resort, not merely a bonus that pays the cable bill and an extra night out to dinner. Even if your wife's income, or income potential, is higher than your own, be wary of the temptation to sacrifice your wife's safety in exchange for the riches of this world.

If your situation warrants this perilous road, constantly watch for the insidious dragons. They will eventually demand your wife's loyalty. Keep on guard, and have your sword in hand. Ask yourself, *Am I willing to risk giving up her undying faithfulness?* God gave her to you and you to her. Let no man, or dragon, put you asunder.

Dragons of Persuasion

This kind of dragon disguises himself in hype. His name is Marketing, and he comes in many flavors of media. Whether they focus on clothes, cosmetics, food, medicine, or even miracles, the airwaves and print media burst with appeals to purchase the latest and greatest. Print ads covered with ecstatic faces, radio blurbs bubbling with rabid enthusiasm, rapid-fire television images showing unbelievably

---

5. Since my wife has birthed seven children, some would accuse me of the barefoot-and-pregnant policy. It's not true. I'm no ogre. My wife can wear shoes anytime she wants.

happy people, and mailers with photos of starving children all work to tug at our heartstrings and purse strings. Are these products and pleas bad? Not necessarily. There's no evil in a new kind of pizza crust, and our hearts should ache over the plight of malnourished children. The dragon of persuasion, however, lurks in the appeal, the marketing tactics that sing a serenade to the female heart.

When God made woman, He poured into her what He left out of most men—sensitivity to others' feelings and sympathy for the downtrodden. A mother, for better or for worse, receives these treasures a hundredfold. When she seeks a remedy for a sick child, she'll try almost anything, move any mountain, and read ten thousand Internet pages to find comfort and healing. She, above all women, is vulnerable to attack because, in her state of begging for mercy, her heart is laid wide open.

Our fair ladies are wise in many ways, yet their virtues frequently cause them to turn from wisdom to false hopes. Salesmen of all sorts, from doctors to nutrition hawkers, promote products using any and all tactics to grip our ladies' hearts, but these salesmen often only want to snatch our ladies' purses. So it's up to us to expose charlatans and defend our wives against improper appeals to their emotions. Check out companies and their merchandise; verify product and service claims. Whether it's a doctor, a roof contractor, or the guy in the ice cream truck,[6] be cautious. By all means, give to worthwhile charities, but screen them closely for integrity.

---

6. Okay. I admit that's going too far. Anyone who has the patience to drive through neighborhoods with dozens of kids thrusting grimy dollar bills at him and changing their minds three times in a split second has to be an honest salesman. But it's better to be safe than sorry.

When your wife gets excited about a new product, service, or ministry, that's your cue to pick up your sword and shield. Listen to her appeal, and force yourself not to wear a skeptical face. Ride with her enthusiasm, but don't get caught up in it. Give her a genuine smile and say, "That really sounds great, Honey. I'll check it out." Then do it. Don't let her down. Her idea really may be the best brainstorm since Welch's® squeezable jelly bottles, so do your homework. If you discover that everything is legitimate and worthwhile, go for it. But if you look under the rug and find a dragon, she'll be grateful that you exposed it and saved her money, embarrassment, or worse. But after such triumphs, beware of a knight's most common mistake, the danger of the victory dance. Here's my story.

Several of my children suffer from food-related allergies or intolerances that lead to chronic sickness and fatigue. Because of my wife's interest in a new type of diagnostic test that purported to identify such problems, I attended a seminar with her in which the doctor introduced his methods. Now, I'm not opposed to alternative medicine, but I've seen my share of quacks out there, pseudo-physicians who make many piecrust promises as they practice voodoo science. Sitting next to my hopeful wife, I remained wary, looking for any sign of quackery. Much of the nutritional information the doctor gave us rang true: eat healthy food; don't eat junk. Broccoli is good, Twinkies® are bad. But when the doctor demonstrated his method[7] of finding physical problems, in my mind he slowly transformed into Daffy Duck. Watching him carefully, I perceived his gimmick, his way of fooling volunteer patients into believing he had discovered amazing truths about their bodies.

---

7. I'm not going to describe the method. It's possible that some practitioners apply it with integrity.

When we arrived home, I demonstrated for my wife how I could use the doctor's method to find something wrong with any part of her body. It worked so well that I was extremely pleased with my prowess in exposing this dragon. Now, I hope you don't get a picture in your mind of me strutting around the room like some cocky rooster, crowing like an idiot. It wasn't that bad. Yet my eldest daughter, who witnessed the display, did give me the insensitive Clod-of-the-Month award (with all due respect, of course).

You see, my wife was crushed. Her hopes rode high on this doctor's promise, and a cure for her children's ills seemed to be waiting on her horizon. Not only did I dash her dreams, it seemed to her that I celebrated in the midst of her shattering expectations. My wife, angel that she is, forgave my insensitive bumbling, and I promised to investigate further and report my findings.

I learned from my mistake. Kill the dragons, yes, but celebrate their demise in private. Our wives will understand that the marketing dragons deserve to die, but we must remember that the promises they paint on the forbidden fruit die with them. This can bring an avalanche of disappointment.

It's no secret that the world is filled with unscrupulous profiteers—snake-oil salesmen in the marketplace. As holy knights, we're to be imitators of Christ, who was our progenitor of dragon detection. Jesus always perceived the trickery of the scribes and chief priests when they tried to trap Him. In Matthew 22:18, He said, "Why are you testing Me, you hypocrites?" He vanquished religious charlatans with the sword of the Spirit—His Word—and proved His words with His deeds. Let us always be so bold and ready to act in defense of our beloved wives.

This may be a great time to ask if it's right to be so pessimistic about the motivations of men. Isn't this attitude just a form of cynicism? The Bible tells us that Jesus, though not cynical, always remained vigilant: "But Jesus, on His part, was not entrusting Himself to them, for He knew all men, and because He did not need anyone to bear witness concerning man for He Himself knew what was in man" (John 2:24, 25).

Since our Lord knows the hearts of men, we need always to have our minds in a praying posture, asking God for discernment in revealing hidden dragons. We want neither to slay the innocent nor to give free reign to the deceivers. May God help us to recognize these snakes.

Dragons of Influence

M any dragons roam undetected in the arenas of cultural manipulation. They work behind the scenes and manage to control the two towers of world corruption—the news and entertainment industry and the political power machine. In these arenas, they are masters of deception, the rotten apples and curdled milk of our culture who slither from hole to hole in the world of societal influence. Entertainment executives slop the sewage of pornography into our neighborhoods, and they profit from thousands of hours of glorified fornication and adultery on primetime television until immorality has not only been normalized, it has been accepted to the point that opposing opinions are considered archaic and "Puritan." These dragons spill vats of blood resulting from gratuitous violence until the new generation is stoically tolerant of unspeakable acts against humanity, such as abortion, infanticide, and the starving deaths of the elderly and infirm.

Whew! That was quite a rant. And don't get me started on politics, or this chapter will end on page 4,375. Let's just say, however, that political dragons are back-stabbing, two-faced, money-grabbing, one-bit,[8] power-hungry, (insert your favorite hyphenated insult here), wisdom-challenged, boot-licking lowlifes. And I'll leave it to you to discover the precious few government politicians who are trying to make a positive difference.

Regarding their effects on our culture, there is little we can do on our own to stop these dragons of influence, but we can protect our fair ladies from their poison. Home is to be a place of refuge, a shelter from the crazy hurricane of immorality. While we pray for change, write our Congressmen, and/or try to influence the media, our most effective work will occur in the privacy of our homes.

Think of your family as a little island of resistance in the midst of a fierce revolution. It's your duty, gallant knight, to keep dragons of influence from infiltrating your home with their weapons of spiritual mass destruction. Make ready for battle. Here are your orders from the High King:

Get a daily briefing. A knight such as yourself can't always discern the wiles of dragons of influence without steady input from the highest source of wisdom, the Bible. You also can't pursue and conquer these dragons alone; you need help. A daily time of Bible study with your wife and a regular time of prayer are essential ingredients in a recipe of preparation. Make these an absolute priority.

My wife and I have our family devotional time every weekday morning. The two of us go for a long prayer walk, and when we return, the children rise to join us. We read the Bible together and pray, knowing that the importance of this preparation for the day far outweighs that of food, comfort, or an extra hour of sleep.

---

8. I was going to write "two-bit," but most politicians aren't worth two bits. And I already used two-faced, so I didn't want to be repetitive.

Refrain from viewing dragon propaganda. Be careful to close the holes through which snakes can slither into your home. Don't partake of the dragon's media—whether books, magazines, television, or movies—that glorify, condone, or display immorality or gratuitous violence. Even if you believe it won't hurt you, please realize that what goes into your mind has some kind of effect.

Junk food never passes through your digestive system without leaving fat, additives, or extra calories. In a similar manner, immoral images or ideas that counter God's holy ways will leave a mental mark of some kind, a spiritual toxin that resists cleansing. And permitting your wife to partake of these influences gives her reason to see them as acceptable, since you've opened the door to their presence in her life. Or it will give her reason to doubt your love for her, because love never allows an agent of stain to touch a spotless bride.

Engage in acts of counter-dragonism. The best way to counter dragon attacks on your home is to launch your own offensive. But your warfare differs from that of your enemies. Strike back with influences for righteousness, attempting to overcome evil with good. I'm not talking about, "If life gives you lemons, make lemonade." Yours is to be the philosophy of Christ. Love your enemies. Do good to those who hate you. Pray for those who persecute you.[9] If your enemy is hungry, feed him, and if he is thirsty, give him a drink; for in so doing you will heap burning coals upon his head (see Rom. 12:20).

If someone picks a bone with you, don't grab it and smash him on the head with it. Invite him to dinner to discuss the issue. Politely implore politicians to pass just laws and to protect the innocent. Support corporations that sponsor

---

9. Capsulated from Matthew 5:44 and Luke 6:27–31.

wholesome media, and tell them why you're doing it. Good will eventually triumph, at least in the eternal perspective. God has given us this promise. So your participation in spiritual warfare should be carried out using spiritual weapons that spread influences for good, following in the footsteps of Christ, the High King.[10]

Give your queen and squires a break. There's a potential drawback to this protective shield strategy, and it can cause our islands of resistance to crumble and sink during the storm. Overzealousness or paranoia can transform a shield into a smothering blanket, causing resentment and feelings of imprisonment. It can foster extreme naiveté or even ignorance, making a wife or child a sitting duck for the flaming arrows of evil. Simply put, too little exposure to the ways of the world will make our families too stupid to battle the enemy. Their minds will be soft, untrained, and unaware of the dragons' schemes.

How do we keep from rearing pudding-headed squires? We expose our families to the ways of evil in measured, controlled doses. The key is to allow contact, not participation. Schedule chaperoned get-togethers with friends, watch previewed movies as a family, and talk about current events at the dinner table. With each exposure to the ways of the world, discuss negative images and influences, and counter them with truth. This way, the minds of our loved ones are made firm, their swords are sharpened, and our shield of protection becomes a welcome defense against influences they now perceive to be arrows of destruction.

With these guidelines in place, you'll be ready to face the fiery winds of any dragon onslaught. And with your shield

---

10. We learn from Jesus' example of cleansing the temple with a whip, that He was not always a gentle persuader. There are times when a man has to go to war against his enemies.

of defense so lovingly wrapped around your home, the eyes of your lovely bride will sparkle because your brightly shining armor will be reflected in glorious splendor.

Hacking Heads Too Hastily

As avid dragon slayers, we have to be careful not to aim our wrath at normal people who are merely annoying, like door-to-door salesmen or maybe even our mothers-in-law. I realize that most mothers-in-law, like my wife's mother, are wonderful, gentle ladies. Some, however, may bring the portrait of a dragon to a man's mind. They might seem to breathe fire, but they are not the enemy.

Our wives, our children, and even our mothers-in-law should never find discomfort in our sword-bearing ways. We will be like sentinels, powerful watchmen who bring peaceful nights rather than wakeful wondering. Our friends and allies will never have cause to fear our strength, viewing us as prepared warriors who provide security.

Save your sword for the real enemy, the forces of evil that try to split you and your wife apart, topple your faith, and destroy your marriage. As a defending husband, give your wife that security. As long as you keep your armor bright, she'll never fear the possibility of unfaithfulness and never doubt your loyalty. Your defending actions, in word and deed, will prove to her that you're a true, trustworthy knight in shining armor.

4

Choosing the Right Horse

Falling from a High Horse Can Be Hazardous to Your Health

News Flash! Truly humble man found in Saginaw, Michigan.

Saginaw, MI—Long thought to be extinct, a male member of the species, Homo Humilius, has been discovered by a team of researchers in a Michigan neighborhood. Many false reports of humble men have been recorded, but like the Piltdown man, their claims have later been debunked by a battery of simple tests. I asked the head researcher, Dr. Jane (Plain Jane) Knowsitall, about those tests.

"Sometimes it is difficult to distinguish between proud and humble males," Dr. Knowsitall explained in her stereotypical British accent. "The proud male may strut around with gold chains dangling over his overabundant chest hairs, making him easy to spot, or he may appear to be humble, simply dressed, driving a modest automobile and wearing little or no jewelry. You see, it is the mind that determines humility, so we have to test a male with questions that no proud male can answer without revealing his peacock feathers."

"What are those questions, Dr. Knowsitall?"

"The first is simply, 'How tall are you?' And we measure the man to see if he is correct. It seems that almost every man overestimates his height, thus eliminating most candidates. In contrast, our find in Saginaw estimated himself one-half inch shorter than he actually was. There are a few other questions that refer to physical abilities, but I believe the psychological questions are far more interesting."

"Can't you just ask the guy, 'Are you humble?' I mean, if anyone thinks he's humble, he's probably not, right?"

"Oh, no!" Dr. Knowsitall replied. "That would not work at all! You see, if a man denies the truth about himself, especially his humility, he usually does so to make himself look good in the eyes of the questioner. A truly humble man would accede to his humility, but he would wish you had not asked."

Dr. Knowsitall pointed toward a series of charts. "The tests we use are not designed to be crafty. For example, we send a group of candidates out to play a competitive series of matches in which only one man can score the highest at the end of the day. The collection of events is inconsequential: table tennis, horseshoes, or even tossing wadded paper into a waste can. It is interesting to note that while practicing, the men are playful, agreeable, and generally quite friendly. When we tell them to keep score, however, everything changes. Most of the men begin looking at each other in an odd sort of way, as if sizing up their competition. Then, just before the event begins, their faces grow tense, some foam at the mouth, and a few even spontaneously bleed.

"Our panel of judges scores them on various maneuvers, such as giving thirty points for chest thumping, thirty-five for a primal roar, and fifteen for trash-talking. If one man helps another to his own detriment or tries to stop a fight instead of egging it on, we deduct twenty points. Only the man with the lowest score goes on to the next battery of tests."

"Which is?"

"We pair him with a young woman, and he must choose an automobile with her. The car he chooses is given a testosterone-versus-sensibleness ratio by our judges, a factor we call automachocoolness. You see, convertible sports cars and monster pickup trucks simply bellow with pride, while a boxy minivan purrs with humility. Then, he and the woman are placed in the car in the middle of Boston, hopelessly lost, of course, and we watch with a hidden camera in the dashboard to see if he will stop and ask for directions. The young woman is an essential part of this test, because a prideful man is fifteen times less likely to ask for directions when a female in his range of desirability is present. Finally, he and the woman play a game of basketball."

"Basketball?"

"Yes. This is the greatest test of all. It measures the no-woman-is-ever-going-to-beat-me-at-roundball factor."

"I see. And how did our humble man in Saginaw do?"

"During the contests with the other men, he volunteered to go get snacks and drinks for everyone, and then he refereed the matches. For an automobile, he chose a four-year-old Volvo with side-impact airbags. The car had a large engine and a towing option, but we decided these could be quite reasonable options, even for a humble man. You see, strength and humility are not conflicting qualities. A truly humble man finds strength to be practical, not a vehicle for puffing up. Then, in Boston, our subject hired a tour guide and took the woman to see the sights before paying a taxi driver to lead them out of town."

"And the basketball game with the woman?"

"He lowered the nets, asked two children to join them, and the four played a game against an imaginary team of

NBA stars. He spent most of his time hiking the children up to the nets to do slam dunks."

"That's amazing! What was his final humility score?"

"We didn't get to do a final tally. When the game was over, the young woman threw him into the Volvo and drove away. I heard her yell, 'I'm heading to the Justice of the Peace! This one is mine!' "

A Heart of Gold

What is a woman really searching for in a man? Is it a truly humble soul with a heart of gold who casts off all thoughts of self and places the interests of others ahead of his own? Is it a man who refuses to stay on a high horse and chooses instead to walk in lowliness of mind when necessary, a sincere gentleman who declines a place of honor in order to practice humility?

Are you kidding me? Of course not. When I was in high school, I was constantly appalled at how the prettiest girls would hang their arms around the biggest jerks, the guys who started shaving when they were six but never learned not to spit or scratch their crotches in public. These apes of society kissed and caressed their girlfriends when they were around and then bragged about their sexual conquests when they were with "the guys," even insulting their "girlfriends" just to flaunt their macho disconnection. As I watched their antics, they became like mocking monkeys, swinging by long hairy arms, howling in harmony, and throwing dung around their cage. Is this what a woman really wants?

There is a sad truth in life and relationships. Precious few women really know what a man ought to be. Our feminized culture has relegated men to the back room of society. According to popular media, men are just a collection of baboons who guzzle beer and belch while spouting off sports statistics and hooting at jiggling body parts. They're convenient for protection, procreation, a paycheck, and an occasional laugh. As long as their women can dominate them with superior intelligence and provide sexual rewards for good behavior, men can be manageable, lovable pets. Thank God not all women believe that! In fact, even a woman who dominates her husband may have a deep desire for a man with a backbone, a man of courage who can lead her with a muscular arm while still massaging her heart with a compassionate hand. Why does she fail to find him? A man of such caliber is so rare, it's possible that many women have no example by which to judge. They have the buffoons of television, the shallow hunks of romance novels, and a wide range of laughable masculine role models in movies. The media, which displays villains who use and abuse women, offers imbecilic marshmallows who couldn't keep a house-cat away from a can of tuna, much less defend their women in the face of danger.

Most women, if given a proper model, would seek a man of quality. And, of course, each of us wants to be such a man, one who shows a proper blend of leadership and humble servanthood and possesses a true heart of gold. How do we obtain and balance these crucial qualities, the leadership and servant attitude that shone in balanced splendor in Jesus Christ, our model for masculine living? The answer is simple: We build a model based on biblical principles. But since I'm trying to maintain a knight-in-shining-armor motif throughout this book, I have to shoehorn it in once again and complicate my explanation.

In our knight analogy, the horse is a man's position of authority, his place of power. Mounted upon his steed, the knight charges into battle against any evils within his spheres of influence. Personal integrity keeps him in his saddle, and heroics and godly character give him the right to ride. Yet, even with these tremendous qualities, sitting in that lofty position can be a precarious pose. If he doesn't take care of his attitude, the knight's seat of authority can be a throne of offense. As Proverbs 16:18 says, "Pride goes before destruction, and a haughty spirit before stumbling." A man who takes pride in his power and authority will soon fall from his seat, and the higher the horse the more painful the fall will be.

This is my main point: Choose your horse wisely. Live out your seat of authority from a vantage point that keeps you from feeling exalted in your own mind. The key to how well you ride is how easily and frequently you dismount to take care of the needs of those who ride in the wagons. A horse too tall puts you so high above your family in your mind that you find it humiliating to step down and tend to your little ones. You can never stoop to change a dirty diaper, read a silly story to a giggling daughter, or tenderly hug a crying son. Such acts, you might think, make you too approachable, putting you on their level instead of maintaining that image of an invincible, impenetrable fortress.

Many a man has the opposite problem. His horse is too short. He's glad to be a good servant—washing dishes, taking the garbage out, playing with the kids, etc. But when it comes to leading the family in spiritual matters, making important financial decisions, or going to battle for a cause, he leaves the vision, and the implementation of a plan to achieve it, to his wife. Sure, he goes along for the ride, but he has no vision of his own. He becomes a man on a leash, a playful puppy who's glad to help but who has to be led around to do his wife's bidding. Such a man becomes an object of scorn—a spaghetti-noodle wimp—and his wife dominates him like a nagging mother hen.

"Wilbur! Didn't I tell you to buy maxi-pads with wings? You bought mini-pads!"

"Yes, Dear."

"And you bought rose-dust eye shadow. You know I only use fuschia!"

"Yes, Dear."

"And this bra you bought for me has a hook missing. Take it back to the 'Big Is Beautiful Boutique,' and give the manager a piece of my mind!"

"Yes, Dear."

Poor, sensitive, caring Wilbur would do anything for his lovely bride. Years ago, he wooed her with feelings, playing the romantic who connected with her heart. Unfortunately, in his married life, Wilbur's horse is too short, if he has one at all. He carries no authority, displays no courage, and his character crumbles into the sweepings under his wife's feet. The only steed in his life is the donkey he walks behind, the pompous ass his wife rides while he shovels the manure it deposits at his feet.

How does this situation happen? How does a man go from Romantic Romeo to Mickey Mouse in a matter of months? From Mr. Muscles to a squeaking, cowering rodent? Simply put, loss of respect in the eyes of his wife trashed his authoritative standing.

So, are you a man or a mouse? Are you seated firmly in a saddle, or are you running from the farmer's wife, trying to keep your tail from being sliced from your rear? Let's see how we can stand tall as knights while still keeping our ability to kneel in self-sacrificial service.

A Husband's Authority

A man is lord of his castle, head honcho of his home, main monkey in the zoo, lead dog on the sled, top turtle in the pond, and big man on campus. (Enough, already!) But in practical life, this claim has become a joke in our culture. Society says that men like to believe they're at the head of the home, but women really hold the power. And in many homes, it's true. Men sail along as mastheads on a ship, a wooden face of painted, stupid contentment, while their women stand at the helm with firm hands on the wheel. Sad as it may be, many husbands are often nothing more than ventriloquist's puppets on the hands of a manipulating female.

God's plan of creation, however, hasn't changed. The man is designed to put his hand on the wheel. I'll leave it to others to prove that husbands are so appointed, but granting this position shouldn't be a stumbling block to the majority of you reading this. Most men feel a deeply implanted desire to lead their God-given charges, and as long as husbands aren't drooling ogres with sledgehammers, most wives don't have a problem with submitting to their leadership. What each man needs is a set of guidelines for establishing authority and carrying out his high calling without slipping into the habits of ogreness.[1]

Since a man's authority is granted by God, the first lesson is for him to understand his position. He's not the origin of law, justice, and vision; he's merely a facilitator, a conduit of God's authority. In other words, a man doesn't make up the law and chisel it in stone as if he were the originator; he records heavenly revelation and carries it down from the mountain. He doesn't claim to be the author of the law; he establishes himself as its executor or trustee.

What does applying this understanding accomplish in a man? First, he maintains awareness that his obligation is a

---

1. I invented this new word in my language laboratory. Study it, memorize it, and feel free to use it. If your wife stares at you like you're a grammatical moron, don't tell her where you read it.

divine appointment. He doesn't have to worry that his standing will somehow be undermined; it's inviolable. He can rest in the fact that the substance of his position is cared for by God. Second, he maintains humility. No law that he carries out and no vision that he follows should ever puff him up; they didn't originate with him. Although his position is a high calling, he's still just a pipeline delivering God's majestic plan to His people.

With this fact in mind, here's *practical tip number one* for this chapter. Take a sticky note, slap it onto the first page of your Bible, and write this:

I didn't write these words; I just read them.

I didn't make these rules; I just enforce them.

I didn't build the road we're on; I just steer the car.

Now, every time you open the Bible, glance at your sticky note, and you'll be reminded of your place. It's a noble place, a valuable place, but it's nothing to brag about.

As a delivery mechanism, you have the responsibility to mount and dismount your horse constantly, sort of like a pony express rider but without the glamour. You mount to receive and execute God's holy purposes, and you dismount to meet the needs of those who depend on you, establishing communication by demonstrating love. Through this never-ending process of emptying yourself and serving others, you become a model of Jesus Christ.

Unfortunately, a large number of potential knights err by living at one extreme or the other. They either want to stay on the horse and bark out commands as the imperial magistrate of their homes, or they lie low and mingle with the masses, preferring popularity to regal presence. In our culture, as men wallow in feminization, the latter of the two seems to be more common. These men prefer equality in every aspect, and they turn to their wives rather than to God for significance. But abdication of their role makes their saddles more slippery than a greased watermelon.[2]

Many a man has won the heart of his lady with words that tug at her feelings, but if he lacks substance in his leadership, any binding that was created through emotional draw is easily broken by crisis or strife. The husband and wife often stay together, but the woman ends up browbeating the weakling hushpuppy, wishing he were more of a leader. She becomes a dominating battle-ax, and he kowtows in silent desperation.

On the other hand, many women attach themselves to outwardly strong men of low character, and these women refuse to give up on their men even when male ferocity turns on them. The crying hearts of these women realize the value of strength, and they try to pursue the compassion they think must be buried somewhere in those hearts of stone. The men lord their power over the women, who silently suffer at the hands of bull tyrants.

A balanced seat of authority isn't a mystery, although few knights seem to mount its heights. Our culture demonizes strong men as it attempts to emasculate the brave exceptions to the rule. Will you be one of the few brave souls who dare to scale the tenuous mountain of masculine vision? Follow me through a quest of sorts, and let's see how God has prepared a place for a man like you, a knight called to be a leader for such a time as this.

---

2. For you northerners, there's a camp game we play down south in which we grease a watermelon. The camp leader throws the watermelon into the lake, and all the boys dive in to get it. After an interminable amount of fighting over this impossible-to-grip melon, the boy who brings the watermelon to shore is the winner. Usually he's the only one who hasn't drowned during the tussle.

Authority Gained Through Wisdom

When the Lord of heaven selects men for placement in service, He seems to delight in choosing men of lowly position and means. Notice in the New Testament how many young shepherds, fishermen, and tax collectors He chose. He doesn't look at a man's occupation in order to recognize ability or at his bank account to evaluate status. God examines a man's heart to determine worthiness. Fortunately for us, God empowers us to make us worthy, but it's our persistence in following His calling that establishes us as those who will carry out His will.

David, the youngest son of Jesse, served as the forgotten shepherd who was not considered worthy by his father to pass before Samuel the prophet. Yet God sought out David as a man after His own heart (see 1 Sam. 13:14). David developed his inner strength, making his heart one with God's and establishing himself as a man God could entrust with authority, the sovereign rule over His people, Israel.

Like David, we need to incline our hearts toward God. Although God cleanses and sanctifies our hearts to enable us to follow Him, we're responsible to diligently follow in the footsteps of Christ. We are to hunger for His Word, consuming the Scriptures in earnest desire to learn His ways. We are to gain wisdom by plunging into the treasures of wisdom and knowledge that are found in Christ, transforming our minds into energetic workhorses for Christ's glory alone.

Although as husbands we're automatically in the seat of authority concerning our families, we'll have great difficulty exercising that authority if we can't perform our duty as a spiritual conduit. If we don't pursue intimate knowledge of the mind of Christ, how can we expect to be able to communicate His Word from on high? How can we process and interpret a vision for service or faithfully execute His laws with justice and fairness for all?

A knight who isn't prepared for his seat of authority will be thrown from his horse by the slightest tremor. When his wife seeks an opinion from God's Word, he'll babble like a clueless goose, unable to communicate God's wisdom. If he tries to execute justice without knowing God's laws, he'll preside over a kangaroo court, using as models imbecile media husbands who gladly abdicate responsibility in order to obtain quick fixes to their problems. In short, an unprepared knight is no more than a dog chasing his ignorance-shortened tail.

We need not be like that. God has promised a better way. Husbands, if you lack that heart of gold, dismantle your dirty armor and put on new suits that only Christ can give. When He leads the way, don't look back. Every time you plant your feet in His footprints, you'll be one step closer to having hearts that shine like saving beacons.

You've probably read the famous "Footprints in the Sand" poem, the one in which the writer wonders why there was only one set of footprints when times were the hardest. God answers that the single set of prints were His and that He carried the author through the trials. For *practical tip number two,* go out and buy a poster that shows this poem and the footprints. Although the poem communicates wonderful truth, I really want you to have the picture of the footprints so you can write the following poem on a sheet of paper and tape it over the footprints poem.[3]

---

3. No, I'm not saying my poem is better. If taping over the lovely traditional poem is offensive, then buy two posters and leave one alone. Or else, don't buy a poster at all and draw your own picture of footprints.

THE PATH OF LIGHT

It is an upward call of faith,
This shepherd's voice I hear.
Up mountain slopes and unknown trails,
I follow without fear.

The prints of feet still stained with blood
Impress the holy ground.
Into each one I step with care;
By holy zeal I'm bound.

And with each step the prints grow bright;
The darkness fades away.
Though night befalls the wilderness,
My path is like the day.

O Christ, my lord, my sovereign,
Please lead me to the skies,
For in your steps I find the truth
And circumvent the lies.

And if you find me worthy Lord,
Your people to restore,
Let me ne'er forget the steps
That led me to your door.

—BRYAN DAVIS

Once you're on Christ's road to leadership, you'll join in the fulfillment of this prophecy uttered centuries ago:

"Then I will give you shepherds after my own heart, who will feed you on knowledge and understanding.

And it shall be in those days when you are multiplied and increased in the land," declares the LORD, "they shall say no more, 'The ark of the covenant of the LORD.' And it shall not come to mind, nor shall they remember it, nor shall they miss it, nor shall it be made again. At that time they shall call Jerusalem 'The Throne of the LORD,' and all the nations will be gathered to it, to Jerusalem, for the name of the LORD; nor shall they walk anymore after the stubbornness of their evil heart" (Jer. 3:15–17).

God promised to provide shepherds for His people, men who would serve as pipelines from heaven. They would not be like King David, who corrupted the faithful heart he once had. God would deliver a new covenant, one that would depart from the old system—the Law that could not keep a man's heart pure. We who are blessed to live by the power of the indwelling, regenerating Holy Spirit can indeed be completely equipped to carry God's Word down from the mountaintop, to be imitators of Christ in the seat of authority in which He has placed us. His steps are set before us, glowing in holy light even during the darkest nights. Let us follow them with confidence, knowing that He has promised us victory.

Authority Established Through Courage

Although it is God who grants authority, a husband's ability to exercise it can be hindered if those in his care don't recognize his position. A husband's status in God's sight is invisible to a wife; without further proof, she recognizes it only in theory. A godly woman will submit to that authority, placing herself in willing subjection out of an obedient heart, simply because she's obligated to do so. But what if her husband is a mongrel monarch, handing down edicts with an iron fist, yet running from evil like a cowardly dog? Will she be able to follow him with all her heart? A husband's visible elevation in his wife's eyes is dependent on his deeds. He establishes his authority over other people by demonstrating courage in the face of danger or hardship. With a vision of God's purposes clearly in his mind, he can charge into the fray and forsake all encumbrances in order to achieve the goals to which God has called him. Although he's challenged, and enemies rise up against him, he doesn't back down. He's a warrior for truth and goodness, and the mantle of courage dresses him in royal splendor.

Even if his wife has already decided to follow his lead, in order to follow with her heart she needs to see a demonstration of masculine courage, proof that his authority is real in deed as well as in word. He needs to be much more than a skeletal weakling propped up to look like a knight. His inner man must fill out his calling. Once he earns his position as lord of his home, he's far more likely to be treated like one.

For some of us, it feels like an act of bravery just to try to live life in obedience to God in this sin-sick world—playing fair when everyone else is cheating and showing compassion in a cruel culture. But we're called to do more than just avoid the evil the world throws our way. We're not sitting ducks in the middle of a dodgeball circle, leaping away at the last second to keep from getting smacked in the face. We're called to march to the guy with the ball and kick him in the nether regions. Just dodging missiles and hoping that someone else gets hit first isn't exactly our model for courageous behavior.

Simply put, we aren't called to jump in fear; we're called to march, to take the enemies' weapons and break them over their heads. David chopped off Goliath's head with the giant's own sword! With courage as his first weapon and faith as his strength, David used a pebble to crack the

Philistine's skull and bring him to the ground. That's all he needed to bring the ugly brute, before whom all the other Israelites trembled, to his knees. Then, with his authority firmly established through his unstoppable courage, David and Israel's energized army chased away a legion of fleeing Philistines. Such is the power of a courageous march.

Here's your *next practical tip.* Go to a mall and pick up a polished stone, one of those colorful, smooth pebbles often sold in ear-piercing pagodas. Select one that's a bit larger than a nickel. Every morning when you put on your pants, scoop it off your dresser and put it in your pocket with your change. Let it remind you of the courage you'll need during the coming hours. Remind yourself that David used a stone like this to slay a giant. Which giants will you be called to destroy today? Take comfort that God will multiply the little power you have; the mission is really His, not yours. And have faith that every time you use your spiritual pebble to conquer evil, your wife will view you as the sexiest hunk of authoritative manhood the world has ever known. Not bad for the price of a pebble, huh?

Authority Maintained Through Integrity

A knight's ability to stay on his horse absolutely depends on his integrity. Whether his horse is a giant Clydesdale or a miniature Shetland, he's carried by the deeds that prove his character. Some women may not admit it, but a man's most powerful attraction lies in his aura of courage and strength. But that aura fades faster than cheap paint if there's no substance behind his façade.

What gives a husband substance? What's the most important factor that allows him to possess the rare prestige that allows his wife to gladly look up to him as a courageous knight? It's his consistency in living according to God's principles. No man is able to deliver and execute God's vision for mankind while living a life that contradicts the message on his lips. Such duplicity is the definition of hypocrisy, the very root of treachery.

Many in our "Christian" culture deny that a knight has the ability to follow God's commandments. Even the church itself may try to pull him down from his God-given horse by calling him a sinner and contradicting God's empowering victory call: "Greater is He who is in you than he who is in the world" (1 John 4:4). Theologians and pastors blame a "sinful nature" that supposedly dogs a blood-cleansed warrior at every turn, even in the face of God's pronouncement that "those who belong to Christ Jesus have crucified the flesh with its passions and desires" (Gal. 5:24).[4]

Men, I exhort you to ignore downward calls to mediocrity. Indeed, fight against them, for they are the venom of the accusing serpent. We are saints who overwhelmingly conquer through Christ (see Rom. 8:37), and we need not kneel to listen to lying whispers of snakes who wish to bruise our heels and destroy our God-given seat of authority.

A knight's proper horse will be tall, and those who look up to him expect to find wisdom, courage, and proven character. A knight who doesn't possess these attributes can't keep his seat for long, and his fall will bring no pity, only laughter and scorn. May God help us to humbly fulfill His magnificent calling.

---

4. I realize that many faithful Christian readers may disagree with this doctrinal point of view. If you believe that you battle a sinful nature, you can still experience victory. Ask yourself a simple question, *Who is stronger? The Holy Spirit, or the flesh?* Remember, no matter how difficult the battle, God can *always* win.

Showing Humility

Proven character, important as it is in maintaining integrity, can still cause a knight to become unbalanced. In other words, being honest, faithful, and hardworking earns favor, but favor alone isn't enough. A man might say, "I go to the office sixty hours a week, pay my taxes, and have never committed adultery. Doesn't that prove my love?" It proves dedication, but acts of dispassionate service don't prove love. A man who only serves from on high isn't a true servant. He's a benefactor, to be sure, but his attempts to stay above the masses will eventually lead to his fall.

God proved His dedication to His people again and again through the centuries, yet His bride, Israel, kept going astray. God had true authority, and He could have rightfully condemned every wandering heart to eternal punishment. There was, however, one more step for God to pursue, one more avenue that would demonstrate His intimate love. He became a man. He put on our skin. He stepped down from heaven and took on the temptations, the woes, and the weaknesses of those whom He sought. And, most amazing, He became their servant, washing their feet, healing their sick, and teaching them the laws of God.

An authoritative position, even one that has been proven through our deeds, isn't enough. A true leader can't make wise decisions unless he knows his people intimately. Likewise, in order to understand the needs of those in our care, we have to step down from our horses and, in a manner of speaking, put on the skin of our loved ones. When our wives weep, we are to groan in harmony, not necessarily in audible tones, but with caring empathy for what breaks their hearts. When they laugh, we are to delight in their joy. When danger raises fear, or injustice incites anger in our wives' minds, outrage should boil within us as we draw our swords to challenge any forces that would dare to unsettle our precious ones.

Like Christ, we are to wash their feet, gladly casting aside any trappings of authority in order to render service, no matter how humbling. We are to change diapers, take out garbage, and dream up acts of kindness to make our wives' schedules just one second lighter and to keep them from shedding even one extra drop of sweat or tears.

Just as courage establishes a husband as an authority in his wife's mind, true humility and servanthood draw a woman to enjoy her husband's place as a sacrificial knight. He proves that he understands her longings and fears. She can trust him to care for her heart.

It's *practical tip time* again, and this advice will involve action. Is there a job in your house that your wife absolutely hates to do, and when you think of doing it yourself you shudder at the thought? Whatever it is, gird up your loins, hold your breath, and do it for her. Whether it's cleaning the toilet, sorting laundry, scouring the broiler, plucking the chicken, holding down a toddler to brush his teeth, picking fleas out of the dog, or whatever, schedule a time to do it for her. Don't warn her. Don't give her a hint of your plans. Just do it, and don't tell her when you're done.

In addition, go out and buy a bottle of foot-massage lotion and hide it in your dresser drawer. Pick a night when your wife is super tired. After she goes to bed, get the bottle, pour out a dab on your hands, and give her a gentle foot massage. As you caress her toes, speak words of admiration. Tell her how much you appreciate her hard work and willing sacrifice. Let her know that what you're doing is the very least she deserves, that she's a treasured jewel in your heart. The very posture of sitting at her feet and rendering this act of love shows that you're willing to sacrifice, not only your time and energy but also any elevated position your status of authority might generate. You, like Christ, are a servant, called to bring joy and refreshment to your beautiful bride.

The Fragile Balance

Is it wrong for a knight to mount a high horse? No. A knight riding in a position of strength and authority is an essential ingredient in a healthy family. Jesus, our perfect-husband model, rides the greatest of horses, and the Bible trumpets the following powerful illustration of His magnificent position:

> And I saw heaven opened; and behold, a white horse, and He who sat upon it is called Faithful and True; and in righteousness He judges and wages war. And His eyes are a flame of fire, and upon His head are many diadems; and He has a name written upon Him which no one knows except Himself. And He is clothed with a robe dipped in blood; and His name is called The Word of God (Rev. 19:11–13).

The deeds and character of Christ give Him the right to ride so high. He is faithful and true, waging war in righteousness. His sacrificial death exemplified in the blood-dipped robe demonstrates His humility. He willingly stepped off a high horse and shared His body and His heart with His bride, not lording His position over His people. He laid down His life, allowing His blood to spill on His royal robe. What a stunning contrast, the symbolic robe of authority and royalty stained with sacrificial blood!

This illustrates our balance. While maintaining a position of authority in our homes, we are to rule with tender hands. Jesus said to the ostracized Samaritan woman, "Go, call your husband, and come here" (John 4:16). To the woman caught in adultery, He said, "Neither do I condemn you. From now on, sin no more" (John 8:11). He wept with the grieving, poured compassion on the sick, and blessed the masses—Jew or Samaritan, rich or poor, wise or ignorant. For the lowly, the contrite, and the humble of spirit, He constantly stretched out His healing, sacrificial hand. Yet, even in His lowly estate, He exercised unwavering power over evil, sending demons flying for cover, confounding hypocritical skeptics, and conquering sin itself through an act of unspeakable suffering.

As the Bible teaches, "Shepherd the flock of God among you, exercising oversight not under compulsion, but voluntarily, according to the will of God; and not for sordid gain, but with eagerness; nor yet as lording it over those allotted to your charge, but proving to be examples to the flock" (1 Pet. 5:2, 3).

Here is the bottom line, men. Yes, we are given authority to wield in our homes, but the most valiant exercise of that authority lies in sacrificial service. As Jesus said, "For who is greater, the one who reclines at the table, or the one who serves? Is it not the one who reclines at the table? But I am among you as the one who serves" (Luke 22:27). We have no choice but to sit on our horses, but we can choose how we sit. Will it be with noses pointed skyward like pompous penguins? Or will we sit as men divinely appointed, established in deeds of courage and proven in acts of humble service?

Let us rise each morning with one burning passion, a desire to be like Christ. Turn to your wife and whisper a word of thanksgiving that God has so blessed you with her presence. You have yet another day to render service to this beautiful soul, you have another opportunity to mount a horse of authority and draw a sword to lead her through the troubles this new day will surely bring, and God has given you the power to bring joy to one so precious that you would gladly give your life for hers.

Arise, get up on that horse, and do it!

~~✻✺~~ 5 ~~✺✻~~

Choosing Your Weapons
The Heartbreak of Tongue Disease

Sticks and Stones

And the tongue is a fire, the very world of iniquity; the tongue is set among our members as that which defiles the entire body, and sets on fire the course of our life, and is set on fire by hell" (James 3:6).

"Sticks and stones may break my bones, but words will never hurt me" (Author unknown).

Sticks and stones. It's a mournful chant, the pained words of children who try to counter cruel playground insults. Young hearts stifle tears bursting from emotional wounds, and they repeat nursery-room lyrics of comfort while their hearts break with grief. This poem holds no real solace, because the sting of spite burns without physical remedy. Only love will heal that wound, and even then a painful scar may remain in hidden recesses, visited in private during lonely, tear-filled nights.

Actually malicious words are not sticks and stones. They're worse. They're insidious poison, the bites of a viper.

They puncture no skin, they spill no blood, yet they spread corrosive infection through hearts and souls. Few are the unharmed, fewer still the invulnerable. Words carry the explosive power of thought. They are the invisible wind of both love and hate. They are able to caress with healing salve, heap burning coals, and stab deeply into the soul. Why do the most painful bites come from lips that profess love? Why do we shrug off the lies of fools, yet slowly wither and die when a loved one continually slanders or speaks hurtful words? It's the pain of treachery, the exposure of betrayal, the feeling of sheer nakedness when disloyalty rips aside a veil of trust. And what traitor is more deceitful than a man who violates a sacred promise to his wife?

A husband and wife are joined by God through a covenant of loving words, and their sturdy yoke faces its greatest challenge if they allow verbal corruption to enter that union. The caustic acid of an untamed tongue will gnaw at the bond that joins their hearts. A husband's tongue holds the keys to pain and pleasure, and by simple choice he can make or break his lady's heart and thereby the glue that joins them. If he chooses to injure her with words, he has broken his vow; he has violated his covenant to honor her because a sharp tongue can be as cruel as adulterous passion.

We men participate in the greatest of all wars, the daily contest of mind over matter, the battle to tame our tongues. By simply listening to the avalanche of spite in our world today, we feel the hopelessness of the task. Television comedies thrive on one-line insults while canned laughter erupts to remind us that we're supposed to celebrate the humor supposedly found in creative cuts and biting sarcasm. "Innocent" jests that inflict minor wounds have become accepted practice in every setting, from sporting events to church socials. Even the Bible says, "But no one can tame the tongue; it is a restless evil and full of deadly poison" (James 3:8).

How should we godly men respond? We're exposed to a culture of trash-talking, one-upmanship, a false masculinity that's taught and reinforced by every macho stereotype in society. If someone gives a man a verbal jab, he has to come up with a better one. And the man who isn't quick enough with his comeback skulks away as the head-hanging loser while the "guys" pat the glib-tongued winner on the back and strut away.

Coming up with a solution to this deeply rooted problem reminds me of that old television show, *Mission Impossible*. So I'm borrowing from its classic style and creating a mission for husbands.

"Good afternoon, Husband Man. It seems that a wild beast is loose in the dark regions of your mouth. It has the ability to spew acidic venom, causing the rapid breakdown of marital harmony. Your mission, should you choose to accept it, requires you to tame this tantrum-throwing, invective-spitting, complaint-mumbling tyrant—your tongue. Once your tongue begins to speak consistently with grace and kindness, your mission will be complete. As usual, if you or any member of your family is caught or killed, or if you roll your eyes at this ridiculous illustration, the author will disavow all knowledge of your actions. This book will self-destruct in five weeks, at which time you must buy a new copy. Good luck, Husband Man."

Is taming the tongue an impossible mission? Although the Bible seems to construct a hopeless lament, the writer went on to say, "My brethren, these things ought not to be this way" (James 3:10b). And he seemed to allow for success earlier in the passage: "If anyone does not stumble in what he says, he is a perfect man, able to bridle the whole body as well" (James 3:2b).

So how do we solve this mystery? Does the Bible leave us with an unresolved contradiction? Definitely not, as the rest of the passage shows.

> Who among you is wise and understanding? Let him show by his good behavior his deeds in the gentleness of wisdom. But if you have bitter jealousy and selfish ambition in your heart, do not be arrogant and so lie against the truth. This wisdom is not that which comes down from above, but is earthly, natural, demonic. For where jealousy and selfish ambition exist, there is disorder and every evil thing. But the wisdom from above is first pure, then peaceable, gentle, reasonable, full of mercy and good fruits, unwavering, without hypocrisy. And the seed whose fruit is righteousness is sown in peace by those who make peace (James 3:13–18).

The Bible's lament in verse eight can be literally translated, "no one *of men* is able to tame the tongue." The tongue is not like the beasts that people have domesticated. It's an extension of fallen humanity. It can't be bridled by earthly wisdom, because its words merely reflect the wisdom of its bearer. What man can put a bridle on himself? Who will steer the harness once it's put into place? Who will grasp the reins and pull him toward the path of righteousness? A man bridling his own tongue is like a wild, saddled horse without a rider. There's no guide, no taming influence, no way to choose the right path.

In order to tame his tongue, the man who wields its enormous power must be transformed. He needs wisdom from above, an attribute he can't possess without the cleansing flow of divine influence. A man needs God to purify his heart. Once God accomplishes that, the tongue— which accurately reflects the hidden thoughts of a man's soul—will manifest a cleansed mind. In short, the indwelling Holy Spirit *can* tame a man's tongue. He is the manifestation of the wisdom from above who breaks and bridles the savage beast.

Men, did we really mean what we said at the altar of marriage? Did we take our wives' hands, to have and to hold from this day forward, for better or for worse, for richer or for poorer, in sickness and in health, to love and to cherish, till death us do part? In this covenantal bonding, where could we possibly find room for the bite of an untamed tongue? How can its sting reflect the promise of one who claims to love and cherish? Can we, without a twinge of conscience, speak unkind words to our wives and then look at our wedding rings with satisfaction and say, "I have honored my covenant?"

Of course not! And on this truth we husbands must stand our ground. We each established a holy covenant and sealed it with loving words. Shall we destroy it with words of spite or carelessness?

Make this declaration with me: "Neither in jest, nor in earnest, will I use my words to bring even the slightest cut to the soul of my fair wife. I will be true to my vows, and I will cherish her both in word and deed. My words will build up and not tear down, till death us do part, so help me God."

Tongue Disease

So help me God, indeed. Without God, our goal to keep our vows will remain as unreachable as Quixote's windmill-chasing fantasy, the impossible dream of a hopeful madman. But we have real hope. Although our mission to tame our tongues is impossible in the hands of unredeemed mankind, we have a faithful redeemer. The bitter waters of blistering, self-gratifying speech can be purified by Christ, through the power of God's indwelling Spirit. Much more than a wild beast that requires taming, the tongue is a manifestation of a disease. It symbolizes the sickness of sin that the Holy Spirit of God roots out of a man's soul. This same Spirit acts as the rider, guiding a man into the path of righteousness.

Although the dripping venom of the tongue is merely a symptom of a deeper problem, its wagging ways are boisterous enough to deserve a name of their own. We'll call the malady Tongue Disease.[1] It's difficult to self-diagnose, so watch carefully for the warning signs. Do the sounds that come out of your mouth result in your wife's jaw dropping open? Do her eyes widen and begin to glaze as her whole face twists into an "I-can't-believe-he-said-that" kind of horrified contortion? If so, you're a candidate for a thorough tongue physical.

Don't worry. There will be no latex finger probing, and I won't ask you to turn your head and cough. Still, the exam could be just as embarrassing, so take a deep breath and remember that this disease can be fatal to your marriage. All sufferers must identify it, confess it, and seek a cure. The procedure is sometimes painful, a purging cathartic that makes castor oil seem like ice cream, but it's well worth the effort. If your words carry the taste of an untamed tongue, then for the sake of your covenantal vows read on as we explore how to conquer and control this unruly beast.

---

1. I was going to call it prolific papillary profusions, but I've used up all my alliterative allowances. Other people have preferred to call it "diarrhea of the mouth," an eloquent phrase, but too disgusting for gentle readers, I'm sure.

Tongues of Men

The Bible is right, as always. The tongue is certainly a fire, and its flame is often used as a dangerous weapon. A man discovers early on that his tongue wields great power over his wife, doing damage that rips open her heart, making her cower in a pool of spilled emotion. Yes, a man can win a battle by using acidic words, but he'll lose something far more precious, his wife's devotion. The apostle Paul wrote, "If I speak with the tongues of men and of angels, but do not have love, I have become a noisy gong or a clanging cymbal" (1 Cor. 13:1).

Borrowing the apostle's phraseology, if not his exact meaning, I will call a man's earthly, natural speech the "tongues of men." This speech emits words that chronicle a man's self-centeredness—whatever satisfies his appetites, glorifies his standing, or otherwise makes his life more pleasurable. It's a vehicle of fleshly indulgence. "Tongues of angels" speech, on the other hand, reaches out to help others. This speech soothes pain, lifts up broken spirits, and encourages strong souls to excel even more. It's a vehicle of heavenly virtue.

The "tongues of men" speech holds a dividing sword between a man and his wife. It bites and devours. It glories in self-aggrandizement. It's a tool a little man uses to cut his wife down to a manageable size, making himself feel big by comparison. It's a spineless coward's weapon, the sting of a jellyfish. For what real man would ever stoop to belittle the lady sent to be his helpmate? What kind of eel would burn his wife, a woman who longs to luxuriate in her husband's tender words?

Although many husbands frequently cut down their wives in horrible, and even obscene ways, a man who reads this book is probably more sensitive to his wife's vulnerabilities and would probably recoil at such beastly behavior. It's still common, however, among Christian couples, to hear biting comments that are rationalized as "all in good fun," or as jests that "don't really hurt anyone."

Don't they? I remember playing a game at a church's Valentine's dinner in which couples took the letters in "valentine" and wrote a list of their spouses' qualities, each beginning with one of the letters. To my horror, one man invented deeply cutting remarks. "V is for vacuum," he said, a widening grin on his face, "her brain while she watches soap operas." "A is for airhead," he added, "my wife when she's driving." As howls of laughter filled the room, his wife slid her chair farther away from his. The bond of marriage took another blow. Who knows how long the sting of his words will burn in her heart? Tell me, was this a fulfillment of his vows?

Simple, careless questions and phrases are another common form of tongue disease:

"Why isn't dinner ready?"
"Can't you keep the kids quiet?"
"You spend too much time on the phone."
"I'm not made out of money, you know."
"Why can't you figure it out for yourself?"

Each phrase is like the chop of an axe, delivering a dividing slice to the bond of marriage. Each stinging phrase implies that the wife lacks responsibility or intelligence; it disrespects and dishonors a man's beloved. And each unnecessary cut is the fruit of a man's unbridled tongue, the venom of a man who has an unsettled soul.

As these blows continue, a husband and wife drift apart. Trust erodes and finally dies. Hearts once welded break away.

The strife may even escalate to physical abuse after the tongue has sown the battlefield with seeds of discord. Yet, no matter how deep the separating chasm, no matter how far apart the couple has drifted, God can heal the rift. He can destroy the enmity and heal the ravages of Tongue Disease.

The root of Tongue Disease is selfishness. As the Bible says, it's born from "bitter jealousy and selfish ambition" in our hearts. As we examine what we say, we each should think, *Was that sentence designed to get something for myself or to help others?* It's okay to be brutal with ourselves during this examination. It's better to err on the side of suspicion than to casually excuse our words.

Destructive criticism and any kind of insult are obvious forms of Tongue Disease, but other forms are not so easily identified. Listen carefully. Analyze even simple questions. "What's for dinner?" "Who was that on the phone?" "Is your mother coming over tomorrow?" "What are the kids doing?" Each of these questions can be driven by pure motivations, but they can also be raised to satisfy selfish desires. Every one of our words can make us ogres or heroes. Although this is a serious topic, let's take a lighthearted look at how these phrases can be interpreted. Just promise me that you'll take the applications seriously.

Question: "What's for dinner?"

Ogre Interpretation—"I'm hungry, and I want to eat now. And it had better be good, not like that bean-sprout-and-ketchup casserole you shoved down my throat last night."

Hero Interpretation—"Are you cooking something I can help out with? I can slice the vegetables or stir the pot. I remember the cat-and-carving-board incident last

week, so I promise not to spill cooking oil on the floor
again. Did Fluffy's hair start growing back yet?"

Question: "Who was that on the phone?"

Ogre Interpretation—"Who's taking your time when you
should be polishing my golf clubs? Is Frank trying to sell
insurance to us again? If he is, I'll take that ketchup
casserole and shove it in his face."

Hero Interpretation—"I saw you smile. I was wondering
what made your day." Or, "Does someone need help? If
Joan needs you, I'll put the kids to bed tonight so you
can be with her."

Question: "Is your mother coming over tomorrow?"

Ogre Interpretation—"If she shows up, I'm getting out the
earplugs. I can't take another night of hearing about all
her aches and pains."

Hero Interpretation—"If your mom's coming, I'll run to the
store and get that cheese spread she likes to squirt in her
coffee. And I'll put the dog in the outside kennel. You
know how he likes to jump on her."

Question: "What are the kids doing?"

Ogre Interpretation—"I'm in the mood for sex. Let's make
sure the brats aren't around to interrupt us." Or, "The
lawn needs mowing, and I don't want to do it. Who's
available?"

Hero Interpretation—"Does anyone need help with homework? It's almost time for family devotions, so I want to

make sure we're not too stressed to enjoy God's Word and a time of worship."

As we can see, an apparently neutral statement can be interpreted as selfish, even if the words themselves appear to be untainted by sin. Our words might also be innocent or motivated by love. The key lies in our attitudes. My examples may be a bit stretched, but the principles stand. Each of us knights should always ask, "What *is* my motivation?" And as we evaluate our desires, we'll become better able to detect any hint of the ravages of Tongue Disease.

If you discover that your words lack love, you have taken the first step toward the cure. Confession awaits. Surrender to God is near. You'll need another hand on your reins, a hand of unearthly wisdom. Selfishness is of the earth; selflessness is from heaven. Man's bondage to sin came when an earthly being selfishly wanted to be like God. Freedom from sin arrived when Christ came from heaven and selflessly showed us the true way to be like God. A man enslaved to the ways of earth can't tame his tongue, but a spiritual man is endowed with heavenly wisdom, which enables him to be full of mercy and void of hypocrisy. The qualities of such a man naturally flow through his sanctified tongue, for it is a mirror of the goodness that lies within.

If you have Tongue Disease, ask God to purge its source from your heart. Place your sin on Christ as you participate in his death and resurrection. He will make you a new creature, one who can cleanse every motivation as it congeals into spoken words. Your voice will become a tool of blessing, a tongue of angels bathed in love. Even your covenantal bond of marriage will be renewed. Your newly tamed tongue will reinforce the vows it so recently disparaged, crucifying an old way of life that God Himself will cast away into the sea of forgetfulness. May God help your wife heal from those wounds, forgive your past, and remember your cutting words no more.

Tongues of Angels

Your words are the most powerful balm you can offer. You have the ability to caress your wife's heart with soothing love—the rich, healing touch of tender words. With every utterance, you should seek to make your voice a warm blanket, a curative salve, an uplifting arm, or an encouraging pat on the back. Every moment is an opportunity to build up your wife. With your sanctified tongue you can always keep your home verbally blessed, and as you do, you will be reaffirming your vows daily.

Let's look at a practical example of how we knights can exercise our angelic tongues. Let's say a guy goes to his dresser drawer and notices that there's no clean underwear. What should he say? I'll give four possibilities, with a rating for each.

Contemptible: "Where's my underwear? Can't you ever turn off the television and get some work done around here for a change?"

Any husband who would utter this tirade deserves to be tied up, doused in fish oil, and thrown into a yard with a hundred feral cats. Don't ever say anything remotely like this.

Awful: "Why can't you keep clean underwear in my drawer?"

This accusing statement implies that the wife is unable to keep up with a sacred duty that chauvinists have etched in stone, "Women do laundry." Such men think that laundry duty is in the commandments somewhere, probably right next to this one: "Men get to rest and watch television after a meal while women do the dishes."

Still lacking: "I don't have any clean underwear. Is the washing machine broken?"

This statement is better, but it contains a fatal flaw. Although the husband verbally directs his doubts toward the machine, he's still focusing on his own needs rather than those of his wife. His desire is to get clean underwear, no matter who or what is to blame. In his mind, the blame would still rest squarely on his wife because she didn't call the repairman to get the machine fixed.

Commendable: "I get the feeling you're overworked, Sweetheart. I'll draw a nice tub of bathwater and pour in some skin softeners. I'll also put on that Vivaldi music you like, and while you soak, I'll do the rest of the laundry."

Upon noticing his lack of underwear, this husband's first thought is for the well-being of his wife. He knows and trusts her character. If she hasn't had a chance to do laundry, then it's certainly no fault of hers. In fact, why hasn't he (lazy bum!) pitched in and done it himself? Well, he'll just fix that right here and now! With complete sincerity, he sees to the comfort of his overworked wife and does the work she was unable to complete.

Should he mention the laundry at all? Absolutely! Although raising the issue carries the risk of making his wife feel bad, it will help her to realize that her husband is on her side. He understands that household chores aren't hers alone, and she'll be gratified to see him chip in. Also, if she *is* a bit lazy, she'll become aware of her deficiency through gentle means, and her husband's loving response should arouse a desire to please him.

We could go over a hundred examples of situations in which you have an opportunity to speak with grace, and the same principles would underlie each one:

1. Utter no word that focuses on your needs.
2. Avoid directly exposing a deficiency in your wife.
3. Investigate solving a problem yourself.
4. If you can't think of a way to solve a problem without pointing it out, make your first statement a blessing. Offer encouragement and a compliment before you raise an objection.
5. Never scold. Let your speech flow in tenderness, lavishing your wife with grace and mercy.
6. Make sure that your actions match your words. Provide practical help in keeping with verbal blessings you give.

As we knights learn to react to every situation with a blessing rather than a curse, we'll gain an angelic aura in our wives' eyes. Our armor will never be brighter than when our tongues deliver only words of peace and love. The bond of covenantal unity will never be broken as long as our deeds and words reinforce our wedding day promises and our wives respond in kind.

Tongues of Devils

Although you've trained (or are in the process of training) your tongue to utter kind words, sometimes you must use it as a defensive weapon against forces of darkness. I raise this topic with trepidation, remembering the Bible's warning to be infants in evil (see 1 Cor. 14:20) as we venture into understanding the ways of the most deadly use of spoken language—the sin of verbal treachery, the poisonous twin sisters, slander and gossip.

Sinful influences readily use the tongue as a destructive torch, a raging inferno that destroys the reputations of even the most upright men and women. We are not to participate in the deeds of darkness (see Eph. 5:11), but exposing them requires the ability to discern their presence and battle their assaults. In other words, if we don't know evil is approaching, it can easily stab our wives or us in the back.

I bring this warning, husbands, because part of our duty is to guard our wives from harm. It's part of our covenantal vow. Although the power of God can tame our tongues, the tongues of others may infiltrate our homes and bring with them the fiery darts of Satan. One of the greatest sins is the evil of gossip. Although men often participate, the female gender is more susceptible to gossip's allure. As Paul taught, speaking of young widows, "At the same time they also learn to be idle, as they go around from house to house; and not merely idle, but also gossips and busybodies, talking about things not proper to mention" (1 Tim. 5:13). These busy tongues, excited by burning news, search for ears waiting to be tickled, and the very act of broadcasting a headline builds them up as "women in the know." Their importance swells along with their pride, and their appetite for tattling tidbits grows insatiable as they forage the countryside for tasty gossip.

"Just so you'll know how to pray for Madge," the wagging tongue begins, "her husband is being indicted for tax evasion. And you'll never guess what else."

"What?" the tickled ear's owner replies.

"The bank is foreclosing on their house. I knew they went in over their heads when they bought that mansion. Why, I told Madge yesterday . . ."

And so it goes. In the guise of updating prayer requests or simply spreading "important" news, idle women feign sensitivity to others. Whether veiled in façades of compassion or openly cutting with brazen tongues, these gossips build up their own images on the backs of fallen competitors. Sometimes their busy tongues bear truth, but no man or woman has an inherent right to intimate knowledge, especially when the facts tear down someone's reputation. The tongues may also carry lies that bring discouragement, chisel away at faith, and betray friends.

"Oh, you know Madge. She wouldn't tell you about her husband. She told me she never trusted you anyway. I'm just glad I was here to warn you. Otherwise, you wouldn't know she was biting your back when you're not around."

It might be slander; it might be a lie wrapped in cellophane truth. The busybody might be relating unadulterated facts, but if the message carries even a hint of tearing down, it's gossip. It's the seed of destruction. It's the poison of the devil's tongue.

Knights, we must do everything possible to guard our wives from these busybodies, never allowing words of gossip to come into our ears without a challenge. If we recognize one of these cackling hens or roosters, we are to boldly draw our righteous swords and expose the dark deed, ensuring that our speech is full of grace but making our point clear.

"Uh, excuse me, Jezebel. We don't wish to discuss this here. We'll call Madge right now and see if we can help her, but we will not exchange gossip, nor will we entertain your destructive opinions. You're welcome in our house as a friend, but if you persist in spreading your slander I will ask you to leave."

I know that this may sound harsh or overly eloquent, but it's better than, "Begone, evil seductress, or I will cut out your tongue and feed it to the gerbils!" Whatever words you choose, remember that gossips are not easily cowed. They seek to cause injury and hope to pollute our wives (or us) with seductive influences. It may be time to sharpen our tongues and use them as defensive weapons, as did Christ when He said to the tempter, "Begone, Satan" (Matt. 4:10) and to the Pharisees, "You are of your father the devil" (John 8:44).

By ridding our homes of this destructive influence, we shield our wives from impure thoughts and suppress the division that gossip always carries. We protect them from the temptation of carrying a burning brand that begs to be transported to another easily tickled ear. We demonstrate our willingness to use our tongues to battle and conquer evil, thereby solidifying the holy bond with our wives as we follow our covenantal promise to protect them from harm.

In conclusion, knight, remember that your tongue is powerful, too powerful for you to control without the indwelling Spirit of God. And once trained, your tongue can share words that become passionate messages of love. Lavish your wife with grace. Bathe her in kindness. But never forget to keep your sword sharp in order to defend her against evil.

A tamed tongue is possible with God in control. I know it sounds gross, but your tongue can keep your armor shining. Trust me, it won't leave a bad taste in your mouth.

6

The Knight's Code
Inviolable, Unbreakable, Immutable, and Other Sacred Synonyms

There are many codes of conduct we follow in our culture, both written and unwritten. Some are so inviolable most of us would shudder even at the thought of breaking the code. Would we ridicule a crying child who has just lost his parents? Would we trip up a blind man who taps his cane on the sidewalk? Of course not.

Yet society embraces other behavior codes in principle while winking at those who violate them. There is little if any outrage expressed toward a motorist who breaks the speed limit, a taxpayer who inflates his deductions, or a store customer who notices the extra change he receives and pockets it for himself. Why? Because, "Everyone's doing it." Or, as some might say, "Nobody's perfect."

We live in a culture of excuses. "Pardon me for breaking my promise," so many cry, "I'm only human." And with this lame apology, many vows of fidelity are tossed away like yesterday's newspaper, valuable and fresh one day, a birdcage lining the next. A man shatters a code of conduct without

fear of retribution, because his fellows nod their understanding of his weaknesses.

Many churches today join those nodding heads, accept-
ing sin as normal because of perceived spiritual frailty in
redeemed men. They hold to a form of godliness but deny
its power, thereby acquiescing to the common notion that
men are unable to control their desires, even with the power
of God dwelling within. They state with undying confidence,
"We're just sinners saved by grace."

Husbands, we need not conform to this weak, faithless
confession. We can be so much more than the spineless men
that many churches of today expect us to be. We believe that
God gives us the power to honor the laws he lays down, to
follow the path he calls us to tread. The code of conduct
that God has established for us shines as a bright light in a
world that condones darkness. God's plan for men is established on the foundation of Christ our perfect model, built
with the bricks of men who are unafraid to flex their God-
given muscles, and held together by the mortar of masculine courage. With faith in God's promises, we can follow
that code. We can change the world.

I chose "knights in shining armor" as my ongoing illustration because of the magnificence of the legendary code
of the knights, a system of character and conduct to which
the warriors of old promised to adhere. The Old Code, as it
is called in modern times, was based on the Bible's description of a real man, the image of godly masculinity. It captures, in effect, the chivalry of days gone by.

Although popular media have attempted to canonize the
Old Code in songs and poems, no ancient document, as far
as I know, spells it out word for word. Therefore I will sum-
marize it, having gleaned the code's principles from several
authoritative sources. Remember, this is serious stuff. To follow the Bible's guidelines for victory in Christ is the most

important exhortation I can give, and without confidence in the faithfulness of God to deliver us from bondage to sin, we are doomed to fail in our quest to be men of God.

So now I present the code of a knight, a biblical blueprint for every husband who seeks to reach the pinnacle of God's favor. It presents an extraordinary challenge, but we have been endowed with a Spirit who enables us to overcome. This blueprint is visionary, but because we have been given insight we can see its fulfillment. It lies beyond the goals most people set, but we have been equipped to reach out and grasp the joy of freedom from sin's bondage. We can all live this life victoriously, because we are more than conquerors in Christ (see Rom. 8:37).

A Knight's Discipline and Preparation

1. A knight exercises his body in order to increase and maintain his strength. Without bodily discipline, he will not be able to defend those within his fold of protection.

Most men enjoy the thought of having muscular bodies, bulging biceps, rock hard abs, and pectorals that make their shirts bulge at chest level rather than over their belts. But for the majority, it's just a dream. As the mind wanders into what it takes to get those muscles—gut-busting labor, hours of sweaty, lung-piercing agony, refusing a second slice of Boston cream pie—many men realize why they don't already have that kind of body. It's hard work! It hurts, especially missing out on extra pie!

As they say, "No pain, no gain." The desires of the body are powerful, both in what it yearns for and what it cries out against. When the desires of the flesh rule the mind, the body relaxes, eats whatever it wants, and disdains exercise. It becomes flabby, and it drags the mind down with it, resulting in complete laziness and a Jell-O® mind in a Crisco® body. As Christians, we don't need grotesquely overdeveloped Mr. Universe bodies. We need strength, tone, and physical vigor. We, like the apostle Paul, should discipline our bodies and make them our slaves (see 1 Cor. 9:27). Our Spirit-filled minds are to gain control over our bodies, and the rigors of exercise help us to maintain that mastery. And, most important, the benefits of bodily strength spill over into spiritual virtue as we wake up with ease, face the labors of each day without dread, and give confidence to those whom we protect. Our mental faculties are more acute, and our discipline, by itself, gives us the confidence to rule over the desires of our bodies.

Another bottom line (pun intended) is that our toned bodies will please our wives. No woman seeks to be married to the Pillsbury Doughboy™. Although he's a cute guy in his white chef's hat, and he makes great chocolate-chip cookies, the greasy little gnome giggles when a woman pushes on his cholesterol-coated belly. When your wife pushes your waistline, you want her to say, "Wow! Now that's a nice set of abs!" We can't all be great cookie bakers, but I'm sure each of our wives will be glad to make the trade, getting an "Oh, boy!" instead of a doughboy.

I know some of you may have illnesses or physical challenges, and you're not able to get into great shape. That's okay. Just commit to becoming as physically fit as possible. The goal isn't measured by the size of your muscles; it's accomplished in your mind's control over your body. It's the strength you exude simply because you have dominion over your desires. It's the joy of victory in a world that accepts defeat.

Be strong for your wife; she'll appreciate it. If you have children, they'll love seeing a fit and trim dad. Your strength will give them confidence. Plus, the ability to have dominion over your physical body will allow you to triumph in your spiritual walk. Whether in food or drink, grief or anger, joy or exultation, you'll be able to respond to your inner drives according to what is needful and proper.

2. A knight exercises his mind in order to keep his thoughts nimble, orderly, and disciplined against wandering. Many benefits of bodily self-control parallel those of mental discipline. A brain becomes flabby, in a sense, if it's allowed to atrophy. How can we rightly divide the truth, defend the faith, and counter the wiles of the devil if our brains have turned to mush?

The mentally feeble Christian accepts what he's taught without question. He decides to trust his pastor or a favorite television preacher, no matter how strange the teaching sounds. "Yes, the Bible teaches both predestined salvation and man's free will. I know these ideas contradict, but we just can't understand God's logic." Such a blatant contradiction raises an intellectual battle in his mind, but after this mental midget tries to brainstorm he accepts the pastor's words. He's satisfied with a breezy drizzle instead of a holy hurricane. He is not like the Bereans, who were noble-minded, "for they received the word with great eagerness, examining the Scriptures daily, to see whether these things were so" (Acts 17:11).

We don't need great intellects in order to prepare our brains for God's service. Even if our IQs are lower than our body temperatures, we can still be ready to march as cerebral soldiers in the war against evil ideas and faulty theology. The first step is to read books written by great thinkers— interacting with their ideas, wrestling with their logical progressions, and questioning their conclusions.

A great book to launch such a mental quest is *Mere Christianity* by C. S. Lewis. Although Lewis delves into spiritual subjects with intellectual rigor, he writes on a level that most people can understand. Another good idea is to take time to sample more than one side of an issue. For example, you could read *Chosen by God* by R. C. Sproul, and then pick up *Elect in the Son* by Robert Shank. For a greater challenge, work through some of John Calvin's *Institutes of the Christian Religion* and then read a few essays by James Arminius or John Wesley.

In order to really get our brains into gear, we could participate in a discussion group with other men who wish to exercise their thinking skills. We should choose wisely. We need to be with humble men of controlled temperament who are willing to have their opinions challenged, and who are genuinely seeking biblical truth.

We can also discuss what we learn with our families. As we communicate wisdom, we'll discover new insights or even holes in our understanding, giving us impetus to go back and study again. We must not let uncertainty discourage us. This is to be a lifelong pursuit. Just as our physical muscles will waste away without regular workouts, our brains will return to their former atrophied states if their only form of exercise comes from video games or insipid television programming. With our bodies, as they say, "You are what you eat." God help us if the same is true for a media-manipulated brain.

3. A knight exercises his inner man in order to know and relate to God, the creator of man's spirit, the aspect of man's being that transcends the physical. Without eternal perspective, a knight's physical and mental pursuits will count for nothing. Whether he slays dragons, rescues fair maidens, or even conquers kingdoms, if he dies and rots in the grave he has accomplished nothing of lasting value. Deep down, each knight knows there is something beyond this earth.

A knight's quest for purpose begins in his heart. Being a man of God is a long, hard ride. He needs a reason to endure the saddle sores of daily self-sacrifice and to resist the bitter winds of tribulation. He first looks to his lady, the woman for whom he draws his sword. Yes, she is worth fighting for, even to the death, but like the flowers of the field she will also pass away. Only the Word of God lasts forever, and on the rock of this confession a knight can endure any hardships and withstand any storms.

To build on that foundation, a knight must seek wisdom—the basic source of spiritual nutrition that feeds his soul. Where will he find it? You guessed it, in the Bible. There's no excuse for lacking in biblical knowledge. The greatest source of dynamic spiritual energy in the universe lies between two easily parted covers of leather or paper. It is gift-wrapped wisdom. It is spiritual adrenaline disguised as ink on paper. It is a smorgasbord for our souls. It is ready to eat, tastier than a military MRE, infinitely more nutritious, and, best of all, there are no dishes to clean up.

So, let's study it! If we need help, there are mountains of good study guides and more than a handful of people at churches who will gladly help us to understand the basics of Bible study. Once we're reasonably equipped in these rudiments, however, we should learn to feed ourselves. A man alone with God and His Word is the first step in God's plan for each person who calls upon His name. God seeks worshipers who love Him with all their hearts. And in our quiet places, in solitary communion with our Lord, we will digest the spiritual food and drink that will empower us for His service.

Having firmly embraced God's Word, a knight gains confidence in God's guiding hand. He finds reason to be courageous. He knows that God will always keep His Word, never leaving him or forsaking him. God is his security, his everlasting source of comfort. Although his wife offers many assurances, a knight doesn't have to rely on any earthly source of security.

A Knight's Personal Character

Now let's look at a knight's personal character according to the Old Code.

4. A knight keeps his word and performs what he has spoken. Whatever he commits to do, he will either do it or make arrangements to have it done, or he will die trying. Thus he is careful with his words, using wisdom and discretion with every utterance of his mouth.

A knight tells the truth in a world of lies, remains loyal in a land of betrayal, and works faithfully in a culture of excuses. Even his friends might think he is overzealous, and in this zeal he often stands alone. Yet his peculiar faithfulness makes him trustworthy, even in the eyes of pretenders. His loyalty is unquestioned, even among the unfaithful. If a lie of expediency whispers its desire to be told, a horde of lesser men will stampede to tell it. Not a knight of the Old Code. To speak a falsehood is to spew poison, and he will not allow a drop of venom to leave his tongue, even if offered the treasure of Solomon or threatened with death.

Our culture celebrates the lie. It laughs at the deceptive antics of bumbling fools on television. It elects politicians who tell the most convincing fables. It winks at "white lies" that allow a man to skip an annoying meeting or avoid a tiresome caller by saying, "Oh, I can't talk to him right now. Tell him I'm out to lunch."

And with one shady statement, this man falls from being a knight to being a knave. He may think he's running with the big dogs, but he's really wallowing with the pigs. Whether it's an income-tax "miscalculation" or a "forgotten" appointment, the common man excuses himself time and time again. With each falsehood, his reputation slips into the shadows, where intentions lose their luster, excuses are peddled, and buyers are few.

Are we living in the shadows? What price do we place on our integrity? A few extra dollars in a tax refund? An escape from a pest? A way out of a jam? What could possibly be worth the stripping of our mantle of honor? And our shame is so much the worse if we make excuses, trying to explain why a code of honor doesn't apply to us.

In contrast, a knight of the Old Code stands boldly in the sun. He carries no shame. He is unafraid of examination. The next time you look in the mirror, look yourself in the eye. Can you say without a twinge of conscience, "I am a man of honor"? If you can, great! Now, can you look your wife in the eye and say the same thing? Does she hold her hand over her mouth and start spewing laughter? Does she avoid your gaze and change the subject? Or does she embrace you and say, "I know. And I thank God for a man like you"?

Think about it. What kind of example does a liar set? If you allow yourself to tell lies, which lies will you allow your wife to tell you? How about your children? Will they give honest answers to a man who so casually splits his tongue?

Lying spreads like cancer and envelops an entire family. It spins a spider's web, and it traps a liar in its sticky strands because each lie requires another to keep it from falling apart. A man may begin to believe his own lies, but it won't take long for everyone else to forsake his word. Whether it takes a hundred lies or a dozen for someone to lose faith with other people, it takes only one lie to sear his conscience and make him more able to tell the next. With just one lie, he violates the Old Code, and, should his wife discover his falsehood, his armor is stained in her eyes. Only the miracle of grace and forgiveness will ever remove that mark.

5. A knight keeps himself pure in thought and deed, rejecting association with influences that would cause other people to perceive stain in his character. In other words, he abstains from all appearance of evil.

Although there will always be someone willing to accuse us of wrongdoing, we knights must be careful never to give our enemies a real reason to call our character into question. This application is sometimes obvious: we don't meet our friends at strip clubs, we stay away from bars, and we never wear T-shirts with questionable printed messages such as "Surf Naked" or "So Many Girls, So Little Time."

"But I have liberty in Christ," a person may retort. "I'm free to do what I want as long as I stay away from real sin." Yes, a strong Christian is free, but he must balance freedom with responsibility. We are not called to serve ourselves in our liberty, but to be beacons fueled by true purity, so that, as the Scripture says, "that you may prove yourselves to be blameless and innocent, children of God above reproach in the midst of a crooked and perverse generation, among whom you appear as lights in the world" (Phil. 2:15).

We are to reflect to the world what we really are in our hearts, holy and pure. Our ability to remain unstained in this culture is the light that will draw other people to God. Why risk destroying our reputations by pursuing "freedoms" that are worthless in comparison to guiding someone toward the kingdom of God?

What about our wives? We vowed complete faithfulness to them. Do we display an aura of availability? Do we flirt? Do we spend one-on-one time with other women? We'll cover this topic more thoroughly in chapter eleven, but for now realize that part of our duty as knights is to keep our armor spotless by abstaining from anything that would soil our reputation. The light we shine is easily dimmed in the eyes of others.

6. A knight is humble. He does not boast of his accomplishments, but he gladly exults in the virtuous deeds of his allies because other good knights will not boast of themselves.

If we successfully follow the Old Code, we'll discover that we stand head and shoulders above most men. It's not a sin to notice the reality of our upright character, but we should never let pride sneak into our brains. Without God we would be nothing, nonexistent, without even an inkling of a thought. A man who ignores God, though he rule the world, is worthless and less than a blurry blip on creation's eternal radar. Although we can develop massive muscles, brawny brains, and savvy spirituality, we're still the creature, not the Creator. Walk humbly, men, knowing that we possess nothing that God hasn't given us.

Remember, however, that with God-endowed power we're conquerors for Christ. We can stamp a massive imprint on history. We're rocks of strength, able to forge a radical difference in this world of marshmallow men.

Think about it. A knight in shining armor is not exactly normal, and I'm not talking about any earth-shattering acts he might achieve. When he simply takes out the garbage without being asked, a news crew (complete with a live-feed satellite van) could roar into his driveway to cover this "breaking story." And when he changes a dirty diaper? Heaven help us! There's sure to be live coverage, interviews with his elementary school teachers, and expert opinions from mental-health correspondents. No man in his right mind has ever attempted such a feat of nose-boggling dexterity! The world will lean closer to their television sets as a reporter asks, "How long has your wife been out of town?"

Seriously, every time we make a real sacrifice for others, we'll shine like beacons in our spiritually dark world. How much more of an eternal impact will we make when we surrender every moment to God's will? There may be no cameras, microphones, or blurbs on page fifteen of our local newspapers. Our sacrificial acts may pass unnoticed. Men who sacrifice usually bleed alone. But we seek not such rewards of this world: photo opportunities from media hounds, the massaging adoration of clinging fans, or even a pat on the back from sympathetic buddies. We seek only these words from the author and finisher of our faith, "Well done good and faithful servant." And in these words alone we breathe soul-satisfying sighs. May our Lord always find us faithful.

A Knight's Duty Toward Others

7. A knight seeks what is good for his lady. He never speaks against her honor. He serves her with faithfulness as he strives to meet the needs he is able to fill. He honors the feminine nature, gently caring for a lady as a vessel weaker in physical strength, while understanding her inner courage and spiritual potency. He knows that without her, he has no reason to raise his sword of defense.

Your wife is a treasure. Her value cannot be measured. She is a gift, not only to you, but also to all who have the pleasure of witnessing her distinctive feminine grace. Whether she looks like a model for a fashion magazine or a weatherworn farm girl, her heart is the source of her true beauty. As a knight, you must guard such treasure with your life. Your lady has willingly given up her own potential fortunes and attached herself to you, riding with you in your saddle to whatever horizons you choose. What a fool you would be to consider her a common vessel, an object that's easily scorned and cast aside. No, although she gladly serves as your helpmate, you are to act as her servant, seeking her good, speaking her honor, and meeting her needs.

She is the reason you draw your sword. She is your inspiration for valiant conduct. Hers is the voice that whispers, "You are strong, my good husband! You can do what is right!" She straps on your sword, fills you with sustenance, and prepares your bed when you return home from your battles, weary and in need of her gentle lap. Without her, you might be a lonely, ill-fitted wanderer, without vision, without passion, and without reason to protect those who count on your courage.

A wife is not a plaything. She is God's feminine symbol of virtue. She gives her body to her husband, she gives her mind to making a home, and she gives her soul to God. She is far more than gold and jewels. Treat her like the unsurpassable gift she is.

Whether or not your wife lives up to these qualities is irrelevant. Even if she's a shrieking shrew, it's your calling to treat her as a holy vessel. May God have mercy on you if you have to live with a cold, contentious woman, but your grace, your potent leadership, and your patient endurance will combine to fashion the kind of man who, with God's help, can soften her and melt her icy heart.

8. A knight places the well-being of his children before his own. He is there when they need him, and he never forsakes them, even to his own hurt.

I have covered a man's fatherly responsibilities in my book, *The Image of a Father,* and I recommend that work to you. There you will read the details of how a father reflects the attributes of God for his children. For the purposes of this book, remember that your children will look to you for protection, for guidance, and as a model for behavior. Don't let them down. If you don't spend time with them, teaching them in both word and deed, they will look to other people to find their way in life.

Ask yourself, *Whom would I rather they follow: me, or their peers at school or church? Me, or the images of fathers they see on television?* They will follow someone, and you need to be a man of valor, integrity, and consistency, a man they will gladly imitate.

9. A knight is generous. He gives to those who are in need, and he guards those who are weak and cannot defend themselves.

If innocent people are accosted, a knight will never stand idly by. He will spring into action, ready to raise shield or sword to protect someone who is unable to withstand the onslaught of evil. He is ferocious against the wicked, yet gentle with the innocent, especially with women and children.

A knight seeks justice, desiring the guilty to be punished and the blameless to be set free. He uses any prowess at his disposal to expose evil and exonerate and extol what is good, shining the light he bears in order to discern truth, never using it for self-aggrandizement. Although he knows that evil deserves punishment, he wields a hand of mercy, showing compassion for the penitent and offering forgiveness to the contrite.

A knight walks a steady balance of passion and compassion. He opens his hand to the begging waif and the weeping widow, not leaving their cups empty or their stomachs wanting. Yet he is ready to battle cold-hearted fiends who oppress the downtrodden, turning his giving hand into a fist of war (see Rev. 19:11–16).

Men, what is our response to needy people? Do we give food or money to a beggar in the street? Do we strive to place compassionate leaders in our governing bodies? Do we visit prisoners, encourage the elderly, and send money to missionaries? Do we go to mission fields ourselves?

There are many ways in which we can display our Christlike compassion, taking care to maintain soft hearts within our hardened bodies. The world is filled with frauds who beg for money, and thousands hold out empty hands for food with the same fingers that played video games on the spare television. Don't let an imposter create calluses on your heart. Jesus faced His share of hypocrites, yet He continued to welcome those who came as children to His helping hands.

A knight strives to be the image of Christ, the forgiving warrior. Jesus stayed the executioners' hands when they sought to stone an adulterous woman (see John 8:2–11). He fashioned a whip and cleared the way for praying Gentiles by overturning trading tables and chasing away moneychangers in the temple. And He will come again, mounted on a horse of war, bringing judgment to those who reject God's holy Word.

This is indeed an Old Code, but it isn't fragile. It has stood the test of time because it was erected on the solid foundation of the Word of God. Through the centuries, the Old Code has never been popular; its adherents may not even know of another man who holds to its standard. In the eyes of lesser men, the code's most unfavorable quality is not a specific portion of its grand design or a particular rule of conduct; these men fear the specter of a knight who actually follows the code's precepts.

Legions of men give lip service to the Old Code saying, "Oh, yes, we should all adhere to these principles." But they refuse to believe in a man's ability to obey it. While praising the Old Code's virtues, they discredit the power to abide in them. As Scripture says, such men hold "to a form of godliness, although they have denied its power" (2 Tim. 3:5). They can't seem to believe that any real men have the courage to trust in God's regenerating work.

We, the modern knights of this age, must not listen to scoffers. We believe in the power of God to help us walk in the pure light of holiness. We will not deny the life-giving power of His Holy Spirit as we display the image of Christ on earth. With this profession of faith, we will add the final portion of the Old Code, a verbal confession, that God alone is the source of the power of godliness. While our humility displays an understanding of our lowly estate, our words must lift up the One who has granted us spiritual freedom. God, through our Lord Jesus Christ, is the emancipator. May that confession ever be on our lips.

7

A Servant's Heart
Slaughtering the Selfish Pig

The Heartbeat of a Knight

A single quality in every knight supplies all other qualities. It is the fundamental characteristic that proves to be the bedrock foundation of being a knight, his greatest attribute. It is his self-sacrifice, the heartbeat of his soul. Self-sacrifice feeds all acts of service. Whether a husband respects his wife's domains, washes a load of clothes, or dies in her place, he is motivated and energized by his sacrificial heart—his imitation of Christ.

A selfish man cannot qualify for knighthood. He will never consistently adhere to principles of unselfishness. Centered on his own desires, he will stare with stupid cluelessness at concepts such as servanthood and surrender. Performing acts rooted in sacrifice and deliberate consideration of others will seem foreign. "That's for ministers and missionaries," he might say, "but not for me!"

Most men do fine in the area of self-sacrifice when they first get married. They recognize the need for self-sacrifice, and it usually comes to them easily. As time goes on, however, a husband might drift back into his bachelor ways, thinking more about his own needs than those of his wife. If a man isn't truly selfless at his core, the newness of sharing can begin to wear off during his married life as days become months and months become years.

To the selfish man, the woman who was a dazzling fair maiden slowly becomes "that woman I live with." After waking up with her bad breath in his nostrils for a few hundred mornings, he no longer sees her as a flawless angel. Those new wrinkles that begin to frame her frown may call to mind images of his wife's mother, not the beauty queen at the prom who stood out like a goddess from all the way across the room. For a selfish husband, the desire to put his treasured wife on a pedestal might change to a yearning to hide her in the closet.

Where did the excitement go? Youth fades, passion diminishes, and the desire to serve can be extinguished in the sea of familiarity. Such is the lot of the self-centered man. His inner drive to serve his wife is controlled by externals. He allows his bride to become a common household item in his eyes. His fair maiden, once his idol, is now his ottoman.

A selfish husband can actually relax in front of the television, watching a trout-fishing show, a rerun of *Gilligan's Island,* or some other obviously essential program while his wife scurries around the house doing a hundred and seven different jobs. She has a sticky, crying two-year-old wrapped around one leg, an ironing board under an arm, and an overstuffed laundry basket balanced on her head with her other hand, which also bears an iron, a bag of clothespins, and six Gummi worms. But her "dear" husband doesn't notice. He yawns, scratches himself, and ponders whether or not to ask his wife to fetch him a bag of pretzels and a glass of iced tea. As she watches his self-absorption, she sees an image of how a woman can find great use for a fifty-thousand-volt cattle prod and where to stick it.

The Selfish Pig

B elieve it or not, most of these wretched excuses for husbands actually blame their selfishness on someone else. They have a convenient scapegoat that I call a man's "selfish pig." A selfish pig is the part of his being on which a man relies when he is confronted with his behavior. "The pig did it," he exclaims, satisfied that his actions have been exonerated. He has blocked all criticism by allowing that part of his nature to take the blame. He's in the clear.

The fine art of shifting blame is alive and well in our society. Many men have perfected the art of selfish indulgence by blaming a phantom they consider to be the true culprit. And believe it or not, men who do this may be the most respected, churchgoing men you know.

This selfish pig has a more popular name, one that I'm sure you'll recognize. Millions of people blame their behavior on a concept they call a "sin nature" or "being human." This sin nature is our culture's selfish pig, a destructive stalker who follows a guy around and provides a scapegoat (or scapepig, you might say) for everything from his smallest indiscretions to his most despicable crimes.

"Yes, I lost my temper. It was that sin nature in me."

"Yes, I lusted after that woman, but it was my flesh. After all, I'm only human."

And so it goes. As knights we must reject weak excuses. Every act, every choice for good or evil, comes from our own hearts and minds. Shifting blame is for cowards, scoundrels who would hide behind their mothers' skirts and never have the courage to shed a drop of blood for the sake of righteousness. We cannot allow self-indulgence, the piggish behavior that allows our wives and children to carry even the slightest unnecessary burden. We are better men than that. Not only do we smash the altar of self-worship, we crucify self and all its passions and desires. We bow to our humble Savior, who in bloody-red streams of sacrificial outpouring carved our path to selfless living with nails and thorns. How small are our sacrifices in comparison!

If a man involved in behavior unbecoming of a holy knight has dared to blame his actions on anyone but himself, he has a selfish pig in his life—his personal bogeyman of blame. Such thinking must be stopped. No knight of the Old Code would allow this assault on chivalry. Nothing can stand between him and his quest for righteousness, certainly not a coward's excuse, a theological shadow that shrouds the church in tattered garments of sin. Phantom or not, real or imagined, this pig must die!

If we have followed Jesus to the cross, if we have joined Him in His death, then the old, self-absorbed man is dead. "For if we have become united with Him in the likeness of His death, certainly we shall be also in the likeness of His resurrection, knowing this, that our old self was crucified with Him, that our body of sin might be done away with, that we should no longer be slaves to sin; for he who has died is freed from sin" (Rom. 6:5–7). As the apostle emphasized again in Romans 6:11, we must believe in the reality of this truth. "Even so," he added, "consider yourselves to be dead to sin, but alive to God in Christ Jesus."

If a man has never surrendered to Christ, such a sacrifice can be a painful ordeal. God's work of scouring a man's soul clean of sin may evoke cries of anguish and tears of remorse. But when the work is complete, he will experience the wondrous ecstasy of true freedom. As Jesus said, "If you abide in

My word, then you are truly disciples of Mine; and you shall know the truth, and the truth shall make you free. . . . If therefore the Son shall make you free, you shall be free indeed" (John 8:31, 32, 36).

Freedom in Christ is a widely misunderstood concept. It isn't simply freedom from guilt, which some people have construed to mean "license to sin" and claimed, "Now I'm forgiven no matter what I do!" No! What a backward interpretation! Freedom in Christ is freedom from sin itself. The context of Christ's words demands this understanding. Remember, He said immediately before promising freedom, "Truly, truly, I say to you, everyone who commits sin is the slave of sin" (John 8:34). When the pig dies, the chains of sin are broken, and we can pass along the glorious benefits of our liberated souls to our wives and our entire families. We can show our blessed ladies the sacrificial nature of the Christ who lives within us.

Give and Give

How do we reveal this sacrificial nature to our wives? By living the give-and-give concept of marriage. Some people view marriage as a give-and-take relationship. In other words, sometimes we give of ourselves to our wives, providing security and sustenance. Other times we take from them, expecting them to meet our needs. Although this might seem to be a fair arrangement, it's not the biblical model. It simply doesn't work.

If we give, expecting to get, we aren't really giving at all; we're just making investments with a view to obtaining returns. A man who gives and does not receive what he thinks his investment has earned is, at the very least, frustrated. At the most, he's bitter, perhaps even lashing out mentally or verbally at his wife for not living up to her side of the give-and-take balance.

We, as godly knights, are to be like Christ, who gave His all in bodily sacrifice. We are to give to our wives without thought of return, never expecting our needs to be met. We search out their longings, desires, and innermost wants. Our passion to fill their needs should be such an obsession that we ignore our own desires.

Yes, we do have needs. As men we have physical, emotional, and spiritual needs that our wives can and should meet. God has designed our women to provide for us in wonderful, pleasurable ways. And godly women realize that.

That's where a wife's give-and-give mind-set toward her husband completes the godly pattern. She is to be so obsessed with meeting her husband's needs that she daily casts aside thoughts of her desires and attends to his. In doing so, her husband's needs are met, and he isn't tempted to dwell on any lack because she has so wonderfully supplied. Her needs are also met because her husband has so faithfully sought to fill every wanting gap in her life.

So what do you—a knight—do if you give, give, and give, and your wife doesn't give in return? Give some more. Keep giving of yourself no matter what. So what if the laundry isn't done, supper isn't ready when you come home, and the children are running through the house like savages? Do the laundry. Get some beans and rice on the stove. Round up the children and discipline them. Then go to your wife and give her a blessing, a real one from the heart. Whether she's simply overwhelmed by the burdens of her role as wife and mother, or she really is lazy and wouldn't lift a finger except to eat another Hershey's® Kiss, your response should be one of love and blessing.

A woman who is bulldozed by burdens doesn't need to hear her husband's complaints. Such words of dissatisfaction will work to plow her deeper under her pile of unfinished chores and unfulfilled purposes. He will be like another clattering cymbal in her marching band of worries. Don't go there. Be a messenger of peace. Bring words of comfort, soothing tones of refreshment.

A godly wife who is not meeting her husband's needs probably has good reason for not doing so. There are serious issues confronting her that prevent her from being the support she has been called to be. How does her husband solve that problem? By giving more, more, and more. Without a hint of complaint, he is to search out issues that burden her life and then lift them, not so that his needs will be met but simply because they weigh down her shoulders. He gives, not to get, but simply for the joy of giving. This is true love.

What should a knight do if his wife really is lacking in the support department? What if she doesn't have a good reason for not carrying out her part of the "give-and-give" equation? He needs to step in and lovingly teach her. Helping his wife to learn her role is part of a husband's duty. Such teaching is an act of love; it is the giving of the truth. As Christ gives to us, He also instructs us as to how we should live. A husband has the authority to tell his wife that she has the responsibility to meet his needs.

Does recognizing our needs and then instructing our wives to meet them violate the "give-and-give" standard? Since we are called to ignore our desires and only seek to meet those of others, how can we stop our giving ways and take this inventory? We don't have to pause and count our sorrows; we simply take note of the pain that rises to the surface. You see, our needs are real. If we didn't feel them, or feel discomfort when they go unfulfilled, they wouldn't be needs at all. It's no shame to feel longings when our physical or emotional desires have little or no fulfillment. These are God-given drives that force us into togetherness with our beloved wives.

If our focus is set squarely on serving our wives and others, then false needs—mere wants—never surface; they fall to the wayside as we move on with our lives. True needs, such as emotional and physical closeness with our wives and tender bonding, will eventually beg to be filled, and sooner or later, we won't be able to ignore their call. Our goal, however, if fulfillment is unavailable, is to put the discomfort aside, to make our bodies and our emotions our slaves, and to rely on God to give us grace to endure any lack. Yes, there may be real pain. Unfulfilled sexual desire can cause great physical and emotional distress. The lack of intimate communication can bury us in painful solitude. Having to cook for ourselves can leave us nutritionally challenged. In all these areas, we, who are to be willing to suffer like Christ, can endure such hardships with His empowering help.

It's important for a man to let his wife know what his needs are, and once she knows, he goes about the business of meeting hers. If a wife is on board with this "give-and-give" concept, she'll appreciate knowing what her husband desires. But once he informs her of his needs, he doesn't remind her. He again focuses on serving her.

A husband might have to live his entire life without his needs being fulfilled. In that case, what's the worst that could happen? He would learn the fellowship of the sufferings of Christ (see Phil. 3:10). Through serving his wife, he would be more fully conformed to the image of his Savior, sacrificing and suffering without returned favors. In this, a true man of God can rejoice.

Our acts of giving stem from obedience. We are to employ the methods of Christ, who, though he was the Master, became the servant. He stripped off His garments and knelt at the feet of His disciples, washing their filth from heel to toe. Although He deserved the treatment of the woman who anointed His feet with costly perfume and dried them with her hair, He chose to lower Himself to the level of a slave. He gave, knowing that He would continue to give, sacrificing Himself on the cross for people who deserved nothing of the sort.

Although we are the heads of our homes, we are to be servants, giving of ourselves without thought of getting anything in return. We are to take that basin, strip off our authoritative trappings, and wash the feet of our lovely brides. We are to give and then give again. And, yes, it is much more blessed to give than to receive.

The Playbook

What is it like to be a servant? Practically speaking, how do we serve our wives? Most of us enjoy sports analogies, so here's one that hits a home run.[1] Learning how to be a servant is like memorizing our football team's playbook. Based on the need of the moment, we act accordingly, like passing on third and long, or kicking a field goal on fourth and six on the opponent's twenty-yard line. Let's dive into this analogy and see if we can make learning servanthood a slam dunk.

First, in order to learn and execute the playbook, we'll need time and opportunity. We'll also need to learn to recognize the playing field in order to identify where the holes are in the defensive front—that is, where our services will be helpful to our wives. Activities that distract us from a sacrificial mind-set will have to be tackled and thrown for a loss.

---

1. Warning. A gross overuse of sports terms lies ahead. Proceed at your own risk.

Here's our training regimen, the two-a-days[2] of the servant's workout. Turn off the television and leave it off for a week, including football games.[3] Learn the layout of the opposing team's system. In order to be of service, we have to become familiar with the places we'll be called to work. For example, if we volunteer to put away the dishes and we don't know where they go, we'll be of no help. We'll be T-ball batters trying to hit a major league curveball, and we'll look at every dish like it's a bowling ball at a football game. *This looks like some kind of pasta strainer. Where could it possibly go? I'll ask my wife. Strike one!*

"Honey, where do you keep the spaghetti strainer? It doesn't fit in the silverware drawer." *Strike two!*

"This is a cheese grater? With all these holes I thought— What? You'll do it yourself? Aww, Honey. I'd have done it. You believe me, don't you?" *Strike three! You're out!*

The kitchen is your wife's domain, but you'd still better learn the layout. Since this is a great place to be of service to her, learn the field of play. Draw a map, if you have to, with illustrations of various kitchen items and where they go.[4] If you absolutely can't remember where things go, get your wife's permission to tape signs on the cupboard doors and the drawer fronts telling what's inside. Make up a master list, categorized and alphabetized, of where every kitchen gadget and utensil is stored. Here's an example:

Beater tines—Metal twister doohickies that we lick frosting from. These go in the left set of drawers, second from the top, in the horizontal tray.

---

2. A "two-a-day" is the name for the twice daily practices many football teams schedule.

3. Stop whining. You can do this.

4. Just let your youngest child draw them. They'll probably look better that way.

Slotted spoons—Big plastic spoons that look like the worst nightmare of a starving man at a soup kitchen. Who could eat with these? They go in the spatula (see next entry) drawer.

Spatula—Hamburger flipper. Why we don't just call it that, I'll never know. These go in the slotted spoon (see previous entry) drawer.

Tumblers—Short glasses we drink juice from, the same kind Great Aunt Josie uses for tobacco spitting. These go in the floor cabinet so younger kids and Aunt Josie can reach them.

Yes, your wife will change the system all around now and then. Don't worry. It's nothing more than a football defensive coach shifting the linebackers, so always be ready to call an audible.[5] Just deal with the new alignment[6] until you can edit your list.

So what's our goal as knights? To be ready to serve no matter what the need. We must train our minds to look for opportunities to help other people and punch through problems we encounter without throwing in the towel. All the while, we learn to sacrifice and gain greater knowledge of Christ, the One who sacrificed more than we can imagine.

Every moment you indulge yourself is a lost chance to bring a smile to your wife's lovely face. Whether it's television,

---

5. For our non-sports-minded readers, a football audible is when a quarterback looks at the defense and sees something that doesn't fit the play he called in the huddle. He barks and grunts a little differently than normal to let the other players know the new play he's calling. It's sort of like a busy mother going to the grocery store when she's in a hurry, and the manager has decided to move everything around. She hurriedly assigns each child in tow an item to find, and everyone scrambles until the list is checked off—bread, milk, and Oreo® cookies. That's called an edible audible.

6. Asking your wife for help gets you a pass-interference penalty—three extra days of dishes duty.

computer games, the newspaper, a few minutes "to unwind," or a favorite hobby, every activity that offers self-satisfaction is a candidate for self-sacrifice. Sure, you'll still be able to enjoy leisure from time to time, but it's important to train yourself to see these minutes and hours as unusual gifts rather than birthrights. When you finally kill the selfish pig, you'll discover the joy of sacrificial service. You'll find that serving others brings you more joy than any of your old favorite activities, even watching *Gilligan's Island* reruns.

The Death of the Pig

L et's get to the bottom line. If you're still trapped in a "blame-the-pig" mentality, it's time for a change. It's time to draw the dagger, join the festival, celebrate the sacrifice, and go to the altar at which your pig must die. It's time to participate in the death and resurrection of Christ, and allow Him to purge your sin and set you free. The apostle Paul wrote, "But thanks be to God, who always leads us in His triumph in Christ, and manifests through us the sweet aroma of the knowledge of Him in every place. For we are a fragrance of Christ to God among those who are being saved and among those who are perishing" (2 Cor. 2:14, 15).

Men, there is no sinful nature that God can't kill and remove. In Christ, God has destroyed the sinful man, as Paul made clear in Galatians 5:24. "Now those who belong to Christ Jesus have crucified the flesh with its passions and desires." And what is the result? Paul described it in Romans 6:14–18.

> For sin shall not be master over you, for you are not under law, but under grace. What then? Shall we sin because we

are not under law but under grace? May it never be! Do you not know that when you present yourselves to someone as slaves for obedience, you are slaves of the one whom you obey, either of sin resulting in death, or of obedience resulting in righteousness? But thanks be to God that though you were slaves of sin, you became obedient from the heart to that form of teaching to which you were committed, and having been freed from sin, you became slaves of righteousness.

If you haven't yet discovered the freedom from sin that Christ promised, what will you do with the chains you feel? Will you go to the altar willingly, or must you be dragged to the fire? If you want to be the greatest husband your wife could ever hope for, you must take this step. Bondage to sin will keep you a slave to your selfish desires until the day you die, and your wife will never enjoy the benefits of your liberated life.

The promise of freedom is real, and it comes from the lips of the greatest truth teller of all time, Jesus. "If therefore the Son shall make you free, you shall be free indeed" (John 8:36). If you still feel those chains, come to His cross and let Him sever the bonds that keep you from being all the man you can be—the man God has called you to be, your wife's knight in shining armor.

8

Man or Myth
Which Bunyan Are You?

This is Loud N. Proud on boast-to-boast radio. Our next guest is the world-renowned John Bunyan. Mr. Bunyan, tell us your secret to success."

"There's no real secret, Mr. Proud. I just obeyed God, and He did the rest."

"No secret? Come now, Mr. Bunyan, if it's not a secret then why doesn't everyone grow to be thirty feet tall?"

"Thirty feet tall? I'm only about—"

"And how often do you see a giant blue ox walking by? Never! You must have had some cool connections to land that rack of beef."

"Blue ox? I don't have an ox. I just wrote books that—"

"Books! Yes. I've seen dozens of books about your great logging adventures."

"Logging? I have a fireplace, but—"

"Mr. Bunyan, are you denying that your work has changed the landscape in a very real way?"

"Well, no, Mr. Proud. I thank God that my book, *Pilgrim's Progress*, has had an enormous impact on people's lives."

"*Pilgrim's Progress*? My prep sheet doesn't mention that. I see here that you and Babe, your blue ox, performed tremendous deeds of legendary proportions. Why, it says you actually dug the Grand Canyon!"

"Uh . . . no. That wouldn't be true. But I like to think, by God's grace alone, that my book builds a bridge over the canyon between God and men. It tells about a man who went on a tremendous journey in order to find salvation in Christ."

"You mean . . . you don't have a big, blue ox named Babe?"

"No."

"And you didn't dig the Grand Canyon?"

"No, Mr. Proud. My passion is simply to preach the Word of God. Could it be that you've confused me with *Paul* Bunyan?"

"Ahem. Ladies and gentlemen, on tomorrow's show we have a real treat for you, George MacDonald, founder of the world-famous hamburger empire. Don't miss it!"

The Magnificent Obsession

What is this obsession that causes men to cast away comfort and peace in order to chase heavenly visions? There gleams a spark of passion in their eyes, an undying flame that flashes a tireless signal of unfulfilled energy. Like a burning coal in a man's pocket, it allows no rest. No seat of comfort can be found as long as the quest remains on the horizon. It calls; it beckons like siren voices in the night, awakening men from slumber. Many men have heard the quiet murmuring in their hearts, but few have answered.

To follow his quest, John Bunyan chose cold, metal shackles over the warm embraces of his wife and children. William Tyndale suffered fire and strangulation in order to put the Word of God into people's hands. A rain of rocks and ridicule fell on the head of John Wesley as he rode from town to town preaching the gospel of holiness. Through the centuries, other precious fools for Christ[1] have joined these men in their magnificent obsession.

May we all be so obsessed. May we all feel the fire that prods us to perform great works for God. May that burning coal singe our souls, never letting us rest until each day's labors have satisfied our longing to take a step closer to the vision God has set before us. Every true knight has a quest. Every man feels a call to achieve—an inner cry, a restless spirit, a longing to fill a void that aches for purpose. Such a man shouts to God, "Give me service in Thy kingdom, lest I die!" And energized by the boiling serum of potent masculinity, he dons his God-given armor and charges into the world, ready to bleed and die for Christ alone.

Have you ever answered this inner call? If so, does it still ring strong and true? Or have years of neglect suppressed the awakening trumpet that would send you into God's battlefield? Beware, fellow knights. The world's system has cleverly counterfeited God's vision for millions of men. It has satisfied masculine longing in ways that douse men's fire and emasculate their drive, yet it leaves the gnawing void intact. Men all over the world are left strangely dissatisfied, living lives of "quiet desperation,"[2] not knowing why the race of rats has left them with so many questions. For whom or what do they race? Why do they scurry toward a finish line? What awaits them there? Is there any lasting value in what they do?

Have you ever felt that your efforts are futile? Do you now? You work. You sweat. You bring home a paycheck that covers children with clothes, provides tables with food, and

---

1. See 1 Corinthians 4:10.
2. "The mass of men lead lives of quiet desperation" (Henry David Thoreau, "Walden," 1854).

brings sighs of satisfaction to your family. You do your part.
All is right with the world. And yet, it's not.

When you step out into the night sky and gaze at the
stars, cold and quiet in the cosmic canopy of limitless space,
you feel the insignificance of your existence. In the stunning
silence of vast emptiness, you feel your own void crawling
inside, growing and growling, threatening to swallow every
moment of your day, a wasted day, because in view of the
infinite, it has melted. Only dross remains. Whether your
hours were spent in corner offices, on political stages, or in
manual labor, if they were not spent on an eternal vision they
have counted for nothing in the heavenly realms.

Should you strive to provide for your family? Of course.
But provision is a secondary result of your labor, not its purpose. Supplying food, clothing, and shelter is ultimately
God's concern, not yours. As Jesus taught in the Sermon on
the Mount:

> For this reason I say to you, do not be anxious for your
> life, as to what you shall eat, or what you shall drink; nor
> for your body, as to what you shall put on. Is not life more
> than food, and the body than clothing? Look at the birds
> of the air, that they do not sow, neither do they reap, nor
> gather into barns, and yet your heavenly Father feeds
> them. Are you not worth much more than they? And
> which of you by being anxious can add a single cubit to
> his life's span? And why are you anxious about clothing?
> Observe how the lilies of the field grow; they do not toil
> nor do they spin, yet I say to you that even Solomon in all
> his glory did not clothe himself like one of these. But if
> God so arrays the grass of the field, which is alive today
> and tomorrow is thrown into the furnace, will He not
> much more do so for you, O men of little faith? Do not
> be anxious then, saying, "What shall we eat?" or "What

shall we drink?" or "With what shall we clothe ourselves?" For all these things the Gentiles eagerly seek; for your heavenly Father knows that you need all these things. But seek first His kingdom and His righteousness; and all these things shall be added to you (Matt. 6:25–33).

The bottom line is clear. Seek first God's kingdom and His righteousness. He will take care of the rest. All other efforts are merely trappings. Any other vision is counterfeit. A man may be rich, successful, and famous, but if he's not seeking first a heavenly kingdom, in God's sight he's just a giant in a Candy Land world, entertaining but without substance. He's a Paul Bunyan, filled with superficial boasts that evaporate as myths in the perspective of eternity.

John Bunyan, on the other hand, had substance. He understood the call. He knew the pain of separation from the world's comforts and learned to trust in God's provision for his family while he sought God's kingdom with all his strength. Cast into prison for preaching the gospel, he wrote:

> The parting with my wife and poor children hath oft been to me, in this place as the pulling the flesh from my bones; and that not only because I am somewhat too fond of these great mercies, but also because I should have often brought to my mind the many hardships, miseries and wants that my poor family was like to meet with, should I be taken from them, especially my poor blind child, who lay nearer my heart than all I had beside. O the thoughts of the hardships I thought my blind one might go under, would break my heart to pieces.[3]

John Bunyan had a choice. He could have given up his fight to preach the Word and lived without the chains of

---

3. *Grace Abounding to the Chief of Sinners*, John Bunyan, NA.

governmental interference. He could have settled into the easy, quiet life of state-controlled preaching to which so many pastors of his time acquiesced. Yet the call of holy obsession gripped his soul. The call of Christ to bring the liberating Word of God to the captive masses overwhelmed the pleading cries of John's fellows to give up and avoid the crushing hand of an earthly king. Even the pain of leaving his blind daughter, Mary, could not remove his firm grip from the quest set before him.

> Poor child, thought I, what sorrow art thou like to have for thy portion in this world? Thou must be beaten, must beg, suffer hunger, cold, nakedness, and a thousand calamities, though I cannot now endure the wind should blow upon thee. But yet recalling myself, thought I, I must venture you all with God, though it goeth to the quick to leave you. O, I saw in this condition I was as a man who was pulling down his house upon the head of his wife and children; yet thought I, I must do it, I must do it.[4]

John Bunyan sought after one goal, the kingdom of God, and he channeled every aspect of his life toward that goal. He suffered the loss of a wife, and God gave him another woman of great value and strength. Although threatened with poverty and humiliation, John's wife stood by her man. She was drawn by his single-minded devotion to God, the bright and shining armor of a holy knight. And this magnetic charge, the brilliant attraction radiating from a "fool for Christ," proved to be an irresistible draw.

When a godly wife sees the crucified Christ in a man's face, a face firmly focused on the cross, she humbly takes his hand, ready to walk through the valleys of death just

---

4. Ibid.

to stand by his side. Although he suffers shame, she is unashamed. Although her former friends wag their tongues, she holds hers in check, saving it for whispers of reassurance in her man's ear. Although she feels every blow he suffers, she swabs his wounds, ignoring her own, because these cuts and bruises symbolize the pierced hands and feet of her Lord.

Do you want your wife to follow you to the ends of the earth with unquestioning loyalty? Seek first God's kingdom. Seek first the righteousness of Christ. If your wife is a woman of worth, she will take your hand and never let it go.

Let's Get Even More Practical

You may be thinking, *Now let me get this straight. If I seek God's kingdom, I don't have to worry about anything else? If I answer the call to follow the vision, my wife will sacrifice everything to stay at my side? As she commits herself totally to Christ, she'll cast away all worldly loves in order to be mine?*

That's exactly right, men. As long as your eyes are on Christ, you'll never give your wife a reason to be distracted by the cares of this world. With her hand in yours, together you will resolutely follow His path no matter where it leads. Does thinking about such a vision give you a charge? When you meditate on a woman's undying devotion, do you feel a surge of godly manliness? How can anyone say no to such a life, the harmonious communion of man and woman surrendering to God's perfect plan?

But what does it mean to seek God's kingdom? Is this a down-to-earth reality? What are the nuts and bolts of how a knight in our culture can seek a kingdom he can't even see with his eyes? You see, the kingdom of God is not dressed in palatial courts and purple robes; it's not a procession of princes parading in pompous pageantry. God's kingdom comes like the wind, blowing with tremendous power, yet it is hidden from our physical eyes. "The kingdom of God is not coming with signs to be observed; nor will they say, 'Look, here it is!' or, 'There it is!' For behold, the kingdom of God is in your midst" (Luke 17:20, 21).

We seek an invisible kingdom. We are knights called to duty by an eternal king we cannot see, sworn to uphold a code long since lost to the world, and commissioned to take on spiritual enemies that are immune to swords and lances. In short, we are called to a mission that seems impossible. Thanks be to God that what is impossible for us is possible for Him! (see Matt. 19:26).

God's kingdom is a spiritual kingdom. We seek and serve it in spiritual realms. Therefore our daily activities may not display obvious trappings of spiritual service. It's easy to see how pastors and missionaries serve God's kingdom; they deal with souls longing for spiritual sustenance on a daily basis. But how about men who grow soybeans, stock hardware shelves, or argue in courts of law? Are they disqualified from being in the same category as professional ministers?

No, not automatically. A man who obtains his living in a secular environment can still have his heart firmly planted in the sacred. He is a supplier. He fills the streams of God's provision for those who labor in the visible fields. Every minister, missionary, and servant of God who relies on contributions requires a system of support from men who earn money in the world's system. God, the One who moves men's hearts to give, uses the markets as an engine to generate support for His laborers. If every Christian in the world charged into the mission fields, God could surely find a way to meet their needs. It seems, however, that God has allowed some people to generate the funds that feed and clothe those who choose to step out into mission frontiers.

These providers should, of course, share the gospel at every opportunity while they work. They can be effective mouthpieces for God whether at home or abroad. If we're Christians working in the secular marketplace, in essence we're also full-time ministers of the gospel, doing all our work as though reporting to Christ Himself.

> Slaves, in all things obey those who are your masters on earth, not with external service, as those who merely please men, but with sincerity of heart, fearing the Lord. Whatever you do, do your work heartily, as for the Lord rather than for men; knowing that from the Lord you will receive the reward of the inheritance. It is the Lord Christ whom you serve (Col. 3:22–24).

Those of us who labor in the secular realms are collectors for the spiritual, in effect passing a disguised offering plate from which we will provide for our families, our churches, and the ministers of the gospel who rely on us for financial support. Our employment, whether it spotlights us on a stage of fame or secludes us in a basement storeroom, is a means to an end. It should never be our identity or our life's vision.

When I worked in a secular vocation for twenty years I had to examine myself on a regular basis. *What is my vision? Whom am I really serving? What are my real goals? Am I giving my all to a spiritual goal that God has set before me, or am I allowing the temporal goals of this occupation and the rigors of daily labors to blind me to eternal goals? Having promised to deliver my entire life to God for His purposes, am I tempted to allow part of me to be captured by earthly ends?*

In Acts 5, we read the story of Ananias and his wife, Sapphira. They sold a piece of land and laid part of the price of the land at the apostles' feet, pretending that the offering was the full amount they had received. Their sin, of course, was in their deceit, promising more than they actually delivered and pretending to give their all. Were they looking for the accolades afforded those who sacrificially gave? Probably. They sought to receive the favor of their churchgoing peers without making the sacrifice they publicly announced. How far removed were they from the poor widow who quietly placed her two mites into the temple offering! In her poverty and her complete willingness to sacrifice, she slipped her pennies in without pomp or ceremony. But Jesus noticed.

> And a poor widow came and put in two small copper coins, which amount to a cent. And calling His disciples to Him, He said to them, "Truly I say to you, this poor widow put in more than all the contributors to the treasury; for they all put in out of their surplus, but she, out of her poverty, put in all she owned, all she had to live on" (Mark 12:43, 44).

A Path of Substance

Two pennies! Two circles of copper that could barely buy a sparrow in the market, yet they sparkled like gold in the eyes of Christ. Why? As Jesus said, it was all she had to live on. And, as a widow, what income did she have that would replace those two precious coins?

Suppose you had no job. Would you take your checkbook, write a check for the entire balance in your account, and place it in an offering plate? Is your faith as bold as the widow's? Are you as secure in God's faithful provision?

Perhaps God hasn't called us to give away all our money. But He *has* called us to surrender everything to His service— our money, our lives, our souls—and He has called us to do it in a way that has substance, not with mere lip service or with phony portions that represent far less than our all.

A path of substance is a call to sacrifice. It isn't legalistic adherence to a tithe; it isn't bumper stickers, wall plaques, Scripture T-shirts, or Jesus bracelets. It's every ounce of our lives' energy poured out in unquenchable zeal to pursue God's will, to follow the heavenly vision He has emblazoned on our hearts.

We each should ask ourselves, *Does my vision for life originate in heaven? Am I pursuing heaven's goals? If my occupation is secular, am I working for Christ, giving my all to seek an eternal kingdom, whether my offering amounts to a widow's penny or a king's ransom?* How we answer is crucial, not only for us but for our wives as well. Remember, our wives are called to follow us. They are naturally committed to being our helpmates in pursuing our goals, and they will likely behave according to the example we set. Are we leading them down the path of righteousness or into perdition?

Don't forget, Sapphira also died. Although she simply repeated the lie of her husband, Ananias, she suffered his fate—crumpling at Peter's feet, dying in shame instead of receiving the glory she had hoped her offering would bring, expiring as the willing accomplice to the man she had trusted to bring her glory.

Will we be like Ananias, promising more than we deliver for the sake of worldly honor? Will we follow the path of destruction, the wide and well-traveled road to ruin simply because we kept part of our pledged souls for ourselves? Will we, like Ananias, lead our wives to a catastrophic end? Or will we be men of integrity, promising to love the

Lord our God with all our heart, soul, strength, and mind, and leading our wives to seek first God's kingdom and His righteousness?

A woman desires that her moments on earth have purpose and meaning, and she pursues fulfillment in the footsteps of her husband. What will your wife find as she traces your steps with her own? Will it be glory from men and temporary accolades of worthless cheers, or will it be the voice of her Lord saying, "Well done, good and faithful servant"?

Ananias gave for the sake of appearance, trying to impress with showy symbols. He gave only part of himself, enough to show fake godliness, tokens that were designed to fool his peers, but they didn't fool his Creator. And by his application of deceit, he taught its practice to his wife, leading her astray and into a path of destruction.

As knights and men of substance, we are called to seek the invisible kingdom. With driven passion we are to search for the keys to the hearts of men. We would rather bring just one lost soul into the kingdom of God while melting into the shadows of insignificance than to fail in our quest while basking in the light of fame. We are each to cry out to God, "May You be magnified, O Lord! Let me be Your humble servant. Whether called to glory or shame, I am satisfied simply to be Your slave."

The Divided Heart

How complete is our commitment to God's kingdom? Whether we're professional ministers of the gospel or workers in secular occupations, we must be careful how we answer. Each arena has problems and obstacles. Some are insidious, creeping into a man's life like a slowly spreading disease. We'll first look at attacks that come in secular work, then move to occupations normally associated with religious activities.

If you work in a secular occupation, you'll be tempted to make earthly goals your own. You're paid to bring about results that aren't tied to spiritual gain. Whether your supervisor's goal is to win a court case, sell a thousand vacuum cleaners, or stack tuna cans neatly on a grocery shelf, it's up to you to pursue these goals, at least while you're an employee. Even if you're the president of the company, you may still have to answer to stockholders who expect you to fatten the bottom line and increase their dividends and share value. Your time is not your own, and God commands you to obey your earthly master, as we read in the Colossians passage on page 120.

Although you may report to a human master, and your physical efforts are bound to this person, you must never allow your heart to be divided. You have only one master, Jesus Christ (see Matt. 6:24). If a human master demands that you do something that conflicts with a commandment of God, you have no choice. You must obey God rather than man, following the example of the apostles in the Book of Acts:

> "We gave you strict orders not to continue teaching in this name, and behold, you have filled Jerusalem with your teaching, and intend to bring this man's blood upon us." But Peter and the apostles answered and said, "We must obey God rather than men" (Acts 5:28, 29).

But this isn't a typical problem for many godly men in the secular workplace. Being commanded to directly disobey one of God's commandments seldom occurs in most professions. The real problem is usually a slow, unnoticed melding of men's hearts with their employers' worldly desires.

If your career begins to consume your goals, it's becoming your master. And this advance can be subtle. The excitement of worldly goals or simple dedication to duty can distract you from your ultimate purpose, to discover and fulfill the vision God has implanted in your mind. As a computer professional, I worked for one company for thirteen years, moving from hardware and software technician to officer and partner. Eventually I owned almost a quarter of the firm. The partnership's trust in me was unquestioned. I had proven my dedication time and again. As my contributions to the bottom line increased, the company tried to tighten its grip on my heart. My vision for God's kingdom, however, never faded.

Many years ago, I received God's call to deliver a message to the church. During my service to this company, I learned the writing craft by attending conferences, producing magazine articles, and practicing my skills whenever I could. I believed the day would come for me to leave my firm and take my place as a full-time author. I didn't know how God would bring this about. This company would have a hard time surviving without me, and my sense of loyalty begged me to wait for God to make it happen without undue strife. I struggled with my decision. Although my vision remained sharp, my earthly obligations weighed heavily. An entire company counted on me, including employees who would suffer and perhaps lose their jobs if I left.

My tension was real. *Should I keep waiting?* I wondered. *Maybe God wants me to keep working and write part-time. O God, show me what you want me to do!*

In His mercy, God did show me. Another company that purchased ours had their own computer systems, which allowed me to transfer our client data and transaction history during a period of a few months. I then gracefully bowed out without harming the firm. Not only did I have the freedom to leave without guilt, the purchase provided me with money to live on while I pursued writing full-time. I have stayed true to the vision, although the path sometimes seems murky, and God provides the light I need to find my way.

Many of us will stay in secular employment for years to come, heeding the call to earn money for the advancement of God's kingdom. The warnings, however, remain the same. Although it seems that we divide our time between two masters, only one can be our true master and own our hearts. We must never let our dedication to those who deliver our paychecks supplant our faithfulness to the One who delivers our souls. Our hearts and minds should always be steadfastly fixed on one purpose—serving the kingdom by living in obedience.

Those of you who work in religious-oriented occupations face similar tensions. Although your labors are always directed toward spiritual ends, you may have trouble orienting your hearts toward needy souls. It's easy to lose your way in the details of the labor itself. A pastor, for example, is on call for what seems like twenty-five-hour days. If he could just prepare sermons, counsel his flock, and pray for the sick, his job wouldn't be so stressful. But he's called upon to pick out new carpet for the social hall, decide whether or not to serve pork at the picnic, settle a squabble between the choir director and the self-absorbed diva soprano, squash gossipy rumors about the divorced woman he baptized last week, and show up for every welcome-home buffet, kid's birthday party, graduation potluck, and food-oriented festival. Maybe he wonders if the pulpit stage will collapse under his growing girth, for which, of course, he'll be criticized. The body is God's temple, you know.

Pastors, missionaries, and other servants of the gospel are not immune to the forces that try to pull them from the focus of their vision—the hearts of people. They groan under the weight of daily duties that make them feel like servants of details rather than of God. As each stressful labor enters their days, they must refocus their minds, knowing that every iota of effort has a purpose that contributes to achieving God's goals.

Paul is a great example for us all. Although he was a tentmaker by trade, his heart was not in cutting and sewing fabric. He was obsessed only with spreading the gospel of Jesus Christ. Sure, he probably stitched a superior tent, being dedicated to his task and striving to glorify God in all he did, but his mind was not set on tentmaking. His heart was not filled by satisfied customers who sent him e-scrolls[5] telling him how warm and dry his tents were. His passion burned for souls. "Woe is me," he wrote in 1 Corinthians 9:16, "if I do not preach the gospel."

What Is This Kingdom?

Jesus frequently taught about the kingdom of God. "To what shall I compare the kingdom?" He asked. He responded to His own question with magnificent, comparative illustrations that brand the kingdom's image on our minds.

The kingdom of God is like five prudent virgins who made themselves ready to meet the bridegroom (see Matt. 25:1–13). It's like a king's feast filled with guests dressed in

---

5. E-scroll is the early Palestine version of e-mail. It stands for eagle scroll, a message in a scroll that was sent by eagle in order to arrive quickly. The practice didn't last after the first century. Although the eagles were fast, they were too often distracted by scurrying rodents, making delivery unreliable. Recipients also didn't appreciate getting scrolls with field mouse remains splattered all over them. The next century offered the camel express, which presented a new series of problems, but that's another story.

wedding clothes (see Matt. 22:1–14). We celebrate the wedding with righteous living and joy and peace (see Rom. 14:17), not with eating and drinking. It's like the forgiveness of a great debt (see Matt. 18:23–35). It's like the gathering and separating of fish; the good are kept, and the bad are thrown to waste (see Matt. 13:47, 48).

The kingdom of God doesn't consist of striving for riches, because camels pass through needles before the rich find the kingdom's blessings (Matt. 19:24). The kingdom's doors don't open for the prideful, but they swing wide for the poor in spirit (Matt. 5:3). God doesn't welcome those who avoid spiritual warfare, but He stands to greet His persecuted saints (see Matt. 5:10; Acts 7:55; Acts 14:22). God won't confess those who give mere lip service to Him, but He'll give seats at His table to those who obey (see Matt. 7:21–23; Luke 13:24–30). The blessings of the Lord aren't for those who consider themselves to be intellectual giants; they are for those who come to Him as humble children (see Matt. 18:3, 4).

God's kingdom stands as a spiritual home for men and women of faith. It's not for sinners, but for those who live in holiness (see 1 Cor. 6:9, 10; Gal. 5:21; Eph. 5:5, 6; 2 Pet. 1:10, 11).

We are to seek this kingdom, this invisible, spiritual realm of God's love and authority. If we do, God really will take care of everything else. He is Jehovah Jireh, "The Lord will provide" (Gen. 22:14).

Awake!

Knights, awaken from your slumber. Let this be the voice that calls you to your quest. Ask God to instill within you that inner call, that drive to achieve something magnificent for His kingdom. Shout out to Him, "O God, light the fire and let Your holy flame eat me up with passion for Your kingdom! Fill that gnawing void with Your flesh and slake my thirst with the blood of Your covenant!"

Yes, some of you are heeding the call, but I know from experience that most men are content to earn paychecks and let their women take care of all things spiritual. Such a life is not the measure of a real knight.

Lead the charge! Be a man obsessed with a godly vision. Let your face reflect the image of our crucified Savior, and your wife will take hold of you, excited to see the glory of God as she mounts your steed with you, ready for the ride of her life!

9

Chivalry Ain't Dead
Can't She Open the Door Herself?

Husband Man drops a screwdriver into his toolbox and wipes his hands on a shop towel. "Okay, Honey. I fixed the light switch, the cabinet door, and the leaky faucet. What else is on the list?"

"That's great." She scans a sheet of paper attached to the refrigerator by a magnet that features a pizza delivery company. She furrows her brow and silently moves her lips as she taps each item with her finger. "Only eight more projects left. So far you've collected thirty-five points, and if you finish the rest you'll get almost a hundred more."

"Thirty-five points? What are you talking about?"

"Thirty-five Husband Points®.[1] You know, the credit you get when you do the stuff husbands are supposed to do,

---

1. I've decided to claim "Husband Points" as a trademark. Even though it's not officially registered yet, I'm staking my claim in print. I'll be glad to license the use of the term. E-mail me for a list of rates, and specify if you want to use "Husband Points" orally or in writing.

like using Saturdays to fix broken things that annoy me all week long."

"Credit? What kind of credit?"

"In the 'Wife-Pleasing' account. Don't you do these things to make me happy?"

"Well . . . yeah. I guess so. But I'm not trying to get anything for it."

"I know," she replies, standing on tiptoes to give him a kiss. "That's why you get points. If you were doing it to get something in return, you wouldn't get any credit at all."

He touches his blessed cheek and stares at her like a confused puppy. "So what do the points mean?"

"It's just a measure of how you brighten my day. As I go through all the hassles and turmoil of life, my brightness meter takes a beating. You keep building it back up for me."

"I see. So fixing stuff keeps you going, huh?"

"Yep. And not just fixing things. It's everything you do as a husband to treat me like a special lady."

"Oh . . . Okay . . . I think."

Husband Man is bewildered. His wife has come right out and spoken to him in direct Manspeak, not the Gunese she usually dispenses. He feels tempted to ask for more details. He'd like to know how much each fix-it chore is worth so he can concentrate on the more heavily weighted items, you know, the chores that would give him more wife-brightening for the buck. But would that mess up the system? Probably. The details of wife pleasing are a mystery beyond logical deciphering, so he contents himself with what his wife has revealed. He enjoys being reminded that his wife notices his duties as a husband, and he meditates on other services that might generate a whole basketful of points. To see her smile is all the reward he needs.

Chivalry 101

Chivalry—"The qualities idealized by knighthood, such as bravery, courtesy, honor, and gallantry toward women."[2]

Has chivalry died? Has gentility toward women become an artifact? Has the art of courtesy toward the fairer sex fossilized under the pressure of feminist demands for equality in all areas of society, even in the realm of gentlemanly kindness? Have I asked enough questions to get my point across?

Acting with chivalry may be out of style, but it's never out of tune with a woman's needs. Your wife wants to know that you consider her to be a valuable gift from God, that you see her as more than someone who whips up a tasty meal, washes (and sometimes even irons) your slacks, and produces a baby every few years that looks just like you. Opening doors, carrying packages, and fixing annoying problems tell her, in not so many words, "Hey, Baby! You're the cat's pajamas!"[3]

Saying "I love you" and then letting the door slam in her face is the same to her as telling a whopper of a lie. "Honey, you're the light of my life" looks pretty stupid when she's carrying a load of laundry down the hall while you're munching on a PB&J.[4] Even planting a gentle kiss

---

2. Excerpted from *The American Heritage Dictionary of the English Language, Third Edition* Copyright © 1992 by Houghton Mifflin Company. Electronic version licensed from Lernout & Hauspie Speech Products N.V., further reproduction and distribution restricted in accordance with the Copyright Law of the United States. All rights reserved.

3. In keeping with the old-fashioned nature of chivalrous practices, I chose an idiom from a more chivalrous decade.

4. Every reader except those with the most restricted diets knows what a PB&J is, the grassroots of gastronomic delights, the inimitable peanut-butter-and-jelly sandwich.

on her cheek will sting her like a radioactive hornet if she's scrubbing the floor and you're carrying your golf clubs to the car, especially if you point to a tile and say, "You missed a spot." You might as well pull out your titanium driver and whack her in the head with it; it'll do less damage than your mindless, meaningless kiss.

The basic underpinning of chivalry is simple: treat a woman as a treasured jewel, as a member of the fairer sex who deserves your most humble service. She is not an equal.[5] Although you can probably beat her in an arm-wrestling match, in many ways her gender endows her with abilities far beyond yours. And the most important of these is her ability to stick by your side no matter what, whether you achieve glory in your service for God or you fall on your face like a clumsy oaf. A godly woman will stand by her godly man.

Because of her sacrificial adherence to your God-given vision, she's deserving of your absolute gentility. Show your care for her all day long. Open the car door, and help her in and out. Slide her chair out at dinner, and take her hand while she seats herself. Help her put on her coat, making sure each ruffle is smoothed with your gentle touch. If she's carrying a load, drop whatever you're doing and take it off her hands with a smile and a wink.

Yes, women can open their own doors. Yes, they can put on their own coats. That's not the point. When we show them our daily care in the little things of life, they'll believe we'll watch out for them in the big things—problems they can't

---

5. Sexist alert! Feminists beware! I'm not a closet sexist; I'm an out-in-the-open, dyed-in-the-wool sexist, who enjoys the obvious, basic differences between the genders. I first noticed the differences as a very young child, and the older I get, the more obvious they become. Viva la différence!

handle on their own, attacks from powers they can't overcome, and heartaches blooming from tragic disappointments.
A woman may possess an independent streak and protest
a chivalrous act. She may desire to display her strength, even
trying to impress her husband with her brand of feminine
brawn. If she does, her husband needs to take her hand and
explain, "I know how strong you are, stronger than I am in
many ways. But I've been called to be your protector, your
knight in shining armor, your hero. Please allow me this
simple way of showing my undying gratitude for being my
soul mate."

Okay, using those exact words may be stretching reality
to its limits, but a gentle explanation will go a long way
toward melting a woman's resolve to rebuff your chivalrous
ways. The problem, however, could lie elsewhere. Perhaps
she isn't impressed with acts of chivalry; she needs concrete
acts that carry more weight in her home. You see, a man has
to do more than spout a silky speech; he has to show his wife
the truth of his words every day in ways more important
than common courtesies. Opening the door or carrying a
load will make a man a two-faced hypocrite if he's unwilling
to take out the garbage. If he shows gentility only when
other people are watching, his act becomes a boastful play
on a stage. And what good is helping her with her coat if he
won't lead his family in prayer, if he refuses to provide her
with the spiritual covering a man's influence can bring? (see
James 5:16). He warms her body, but he leaves her spirit out
in the cold.

Acts of true chivalry spring from a knight who treasures
his lady. He rises with a blessing on his lips, telling her she's
a delight to his eyes no matter how awful that avocado-
cream mask looks on her face. He sees to her comfort, making sure he doesn't flush the toilet during her shower.
(The last time he did it, she screamed, "AAAIIIEEEEE!"

Thinking she had a leg cramp, he jumped into the shower stall, knocked her on her backside, and began rubbing her calf, wondering why the water, which was now soaking through his "Lord-of-the-Rings" pajamas, was alternating between teeth-chattering cold and lobster-scalding hot.)

On his knees during his morning tribute to the God who molded this gem of a woman, he asks for protection, guidance, and wisdom, and prays that his dear wife may find these blessings as freely as gathering wildflowers in central Texas in the springtime—the ones you see as you drive down Interstate 10, their dainty blossoms making you forget that your kids are shouting, "Are we there yet?" for the twentieth time, and the tape player is screaming a particularly awful rendition of Pinocchio to mesmerize the impatient tykes.[6]

So, whether you're a suave, graceful gentleman or an error-prone klutz, make sure your chivalry is a reflection of your true heart, your way of life as an admirer of your wife's amazing attributes. That way, when you open the door for her she won't look at you like you're a two-headed giraffe, or worse, a two-faced opportunist.

Husband Points

The story at the beginning of this chapter mentioned a well-known but rarely discussed system of scorekeeping, which I refer to as "husband points." There's a reason people are hesitant to talk about this phenomenon. The system

---

6. Okay, so I messed up the poetic phrasing and fashioned a seemingly interminable sentence. But have you ever seen the wildflowers on that highway? Amazing! The bluebonnets are gorgeous, and the oranges and yellows melding with the greenery paint the landscape with a rainbow of spectacular hues. But I digress.

is too often abused, casting surly shadows on what can be a valuable and honorable measuring procedure. You see, the goal of most men is to keep their wives happy. Simply put, wives usually deserve royal treatment. Of course, there are exceptions. In the case of a contentious woman, a husband has to engage in what might be called lioness taming, and the goal is to keep his wife from attacking him should he venture within striking distance.

As your husband points mount, your wife's level of frustration will decrease. If you've been married long enough, you've probably learned your wife's frustration limit, and she needs to release her pent-up pressures. Your job is to read her emotions like the temperature gauge in your car's dashboard. When the needle gets to the red zone, you'd better do something about it, or the cap will pop and the eruption will rival Mount Saint Helens. Her head explodes, and a billion tons of fatal fury zoom past your ducking head. You look back, and a plume of steam rises from her headless neck.

She shouts (somehow her mouth reappears), "I can't take it anymore!" and her well-deserved tantrum is usually accompanied by hair pulling (her own, and maybe yours if you have any), and a fervent hunt through the pantry for anything made of chocolate. After charging her husband and each child with various acts of family treason for making her life miserable, she pops five Hershey's® Kisses in her mouth, foil wrapper and all, and storms out of the house crying something about what her mother warned her before you were married.

Securing husband points is like adding antifreeze to your wife's radiator. As you step in to alter frustrating events, soothing coolness filters through her entire being. Your actions remind her of her loving knight and his gentle hands. She says to herself, *My man is here at my side, and he cares*

Don't let this happen to your wife!
Photo by Lyn Topinka
Courtesy of USGS/Cascades Volcano Observatory

enough to help! Maybe I can get through this day without going crazy after all.

A husband earns points when he accomplishes any of three goals: to make his wife smile when there's nothing to smile about, to keep her from going into conniptions when there's plenty to connipt about, or to lessen her labors when they pile up into insurmountable mountains. We are commissioned to somehow make her Mount Everest seem like a snow-covered ski resort peak, with hot chocolate and a crackling fire waiting to greet her at the lodge when the trek is finished.[7]

---

7. Accomplishing this feat triples your husband points, sort of like a triple-word score in Scrabble®.

Husband points are simply the goodwill that grows between a man and his wife. She learns to trust in his dedication to meeting her needs as he attempts to communicate on her wavelengths and understand her desires even when they conflict with the simplicity of masculine logic. As he succeeds in meeting any of the above goals, his wife's satisfaction with life increases, and her admiration of her husband naturally increases along with it.

But remember, in piling up the points, never seek rewards. Trying to gain a high score for your own benefit is brash manipulation, and your wife will lose trust completely. You will have used her emotional sensitivities for your pleasure, seeking to meet your personal goals while pretending to secure her happiness. Don't do it.

It's amazing sometimes how easy it is to get husband points. Think about the loose cabinet door; you know the one. It has been hanging that way for weeks. All you have to do is fetch a screwdriver, maybe a longer screw, and fasten that hinge back on the frame. Two minutes, tops. Well, okay, for some of us, ten minutes. Anyway, fix it without telling her your plans, and don't tell her it's done. She'll notice. And not only will you get about fifty points when she first sees it, you'll get another ten or so every time she uses it during the next two weeks. Whenever that door swings the way it's supposed to, she'll breathe a little satisfied sigh and think about the kind attention you paid to the details of her domain.

How to Score

Now that I've mentioned actual numbers of points, I'll try to set up a system by which you can evaluate potential acts and how much goodwill they might produce.

Remember, however, that this is all part of chivalry. Honor and gallantry do not seek rewards; they seek to comfort and please a lady.

The first category is simple—refrain from being stupid. There are times when a wife expects her husband to do a chore, especially something that seems simple in her mind, and he stares at her like she has asked him to do something totally weird, like finding a thousand earthworms and bringing them to her in a silver bucket.

"Do what?" he asks.

"When the timer dings," she replies, "take the pasta off the stove and strain it." (She had to repeat her instructions, so potential husband points are cut in half.)

"How do you strain a stove?" (Either this is a smart-aleck remark or pure stupidity. Points are cut in half again.)

"Not the stove, the pasta."

"Okay, how do you strain pasta? Do you call it names, like 'you spineless noodle'?"

(She's not amused. A loss of ten more points.) "No, you get out the colander, and dump the pasta from the pot."

"The calendar on the wall?" (Another dumb remark. This had better be his last one, or he's toast.)

She places her hands on her hips and lets out a huff. "Not the calendar, the colander!" (Hands on the hips are a dead giveaway. It's time for the husband to get in line.)

"What's a colander?" (An honest question. He really doesn't know what it is, but he cringes inside. His wife might think he's playing dumb again.)

Her voice gets more intense. "The bowl with holes in the bottom." She starts talking like she's instructing a toddler as she fishes the bowl from the drawer. (He has become an idiot in her eyes. All points are lost now.) "The water drains through the holes," she explains, pointing to the colander, "and the pasta stays in the bowl."

The timer dings, and she rolls her eyes while letting out a deep sigh. "Never mind. I'll do it myself."

The man digs his hands into his pockets, ashamed. All points are lost. His stupidity has cost him a chance to show proper chivalry to his beloved wife, and she now sees him as an ignorant buffoon, or worse.

What should he have done? Here's the scenario replayed after the husband has read this book:

"Strain the pasta?" he repeats. "Sure. Where do you keep that strainer bowl thingy?" He raises his hand quickly. "No. Don't bother. I'll find it."

"It's okay," she replies, pulling open the drawer. She's thinking, *He's so cute when he tries to help on his own.* (Yes! Extra husband points!)

"I see the sauce is already heating up," he says, pointing to the stove. "Do you want me to make salads to go with dinner?"

"Salad? You don't eat salad."

"Well, you're always trying to get me to eat it, so I thought I'd give it a go tonight."

"No. That's okay. You don't have to eat salad for me."

Whew! "Well, I'll just make yours. I've seen you do it enough times to figure it out."

Well done! This guy racked up dozens of husband points just by avoiding stupidity. And, yes, he would have made a salad for himself and eaten it, too, if doing so would have made his wife happy. Whatever we do, when our wives ask us for help, we shouldn't pretend to be stupid just to try to get out of helping.

True ignorance, however, can't be avoided. If we really don't know what our wives are talking about, we can at least guess, or say, "I'm not sure what (name the foreign term) is, but I'll figure it out." That way, she's likely to help without getting frustrated. We admit our ignorance, but also show our willingness to solve the dilemma on our own.

The second category of husband points comes into play as we each show ourselves to be Mr. Handyman. Our wives may not expect us to rip up the carpet and tile, redo the entire plumbing system, and put the flooring back in better shape than it was. Most of us aren't professional carpenters, electricians, or plumbers. But most women do desire husbands who'll give their best efforts in repairing whatever they can. For example, almost anyone can replace a light bulb, and you can probably tighten a switch plate without electrocuting yourself. Put in a new screw to hold that garage-door switch, hammer a nail where the deck board is coming loose, or place a dab of glue on that splintered wood frame. If you do, your wife will sing your name (or at least think of you) every time she passes by your handiwork. You've eliminated one or more of those tiny frustrations that add to her major concerns throughout the day. Gentle reminders of your care for her will soothe her soul. If you live in a house long enough, the potential for husband points is practically limitless.

The third and most important category is our leadership in spiritual issues. Nothing racks up husband points like organizing and executing a plan for family devotions and activities that further God's kingdom. By our willingness to lead, we tell our wives in no uncertain terms, "Rely on me. I'll lead us to the promised land."

Trust me. Such an attitude will thrill a wife with tremors of glee. This time it will be her love meter zooming into the red zone, and her eruption will be a shower of warm embraces and sizzling kisses. She knows that she has hitched a ride with a real man, a gallant knight who'll take her on an adventure and place the Lord Himself squarely in the center of his vision. His husband points will skyrocket, and her joy will be made full.

Spreading Chivalry Throughout the World

Why is chivalry dying? Is it because of feminist women insisting they can do anything men can do? Yes, that's part of the problem. Many a so-called "liberated" woman believes that a man's chivalrous acts are designed to denigrate her strength as a partner. But that's not true. Chivalry uplifts her value as a woman.

In order to help our society relearn the fundamentals and value of simple gallantry, it's up to us to spread acts of chivalry in every sphere of our influence. As we practice chivalry with our wives, we should perform the same acts for our daughters. Our teenage daughters might look at us like we have a few wing nuts loose, but that's okay. They'll get used to it. They'll also learn how their future husbands should treat them, allowing them to evaluate suitors who seek their company.

Out in public with female coworkers, ladies at church, and even strangers at the grocery store, we can show common courtesies traditionally tied to old-fashioned chivalry. Will some women think we're making passes at them?[8] Maybe. But when we don't do anything forward, such as touching them or speaking in a seductive way, and we demonstrate

---

8. No, not a football pass. If you thought that, you've been watching sports WAY too much.

consistency by showing similar kindnesses toward other females, that concern will soon die away.

Let's open doors, share umbrellas, help with packages, slide chairs out at tables, and show a general, protective spirit. I don't mean that we throw our coats on the ground so women don't get their dainty shoes wet in puddles. If we see a car coming that's going to splash through a puddle and send a shower of muddy goo all over a lady, we don't have to do a kamikaze dive to shield her from the imminent spray. A simple "Watch out!" will do just fine.

We knights have abandoned our duty for too long. Yes, we have had good reasons; many women protested our gentlemanly ways, sometimes with vulgar rebukes. But is that a good reason to cease doing what's decent and good? Of course not. If we work together, we can reintroduce to society the natural gentility of our gender, and women can learn once again to appreciate our gestures as acts of kindness designed to uplift them as treasured jewels.

Reestablishing Masculine Virtue

As we learn to use chivalrous acts to uplift women, other valuable results will be made manifest. Men who learn their proper place in relation to women will once again take up their protective swords, the offensive weapons that destroy both physical and spiritual enemies.

Most men have allowed media and societal manipulation to neuter their stallionesque spirit, to castrate their combatant character. In short, most men have allowed themselves to become feminized. Too many influential men have made statements like, "Don't pretend that's a gun, Billy. It's not nice to be violent." Not nice? What's "not nice" about using force to defend your family? Men in all layers of society have bought into this nonsense. Not only is it sometimes *proper* to be violent, we are *commanded* to be violent when the need arises. We are infidels if we don't rise to forcefully defend those to whom we have pledged our faithfulness.

What has resulted from this rising tide of estrogen, this feminization of all things masculine? Instead of putting away rapists and pedophiles, we slap their backsides and put them back on the streets to once again violently pierce our women and children. Instead of exposing perverts as decadent sinners, we glorify their "alternative lifestyles," thereby legitimizing their sin and allowing them and those they corrupt to march comfortably into hell.

True masculine virtue allows room for a gentle touch, to be sure, but it's the calloused hand of a battle-trained warrior that best caresses the cheek of a frightened child. An embrace of toned biceps brings more lasting comfort than any promises spoken from Mommy's rocking chair. It takes a strong shepherd of true gallantry to soothe the fears of his shivering lambs.

Knights, we are not starry-eyed mothers who believe in the best intentions of mankind. We are realists who understand the evil purposes of evil men, and we are commissioned to expose deeds of darkness that invade our spheres of protection (see Eph. 5:11.) As we restore our position as the masculine shepherds of society, we will see a radical transformation for the better, as long as our warrior spirits are tamed by the love of Jesus Christ.

Romance: The Final Frontier

A re men romantically challenged? Do men have a natural counterattraction when it comes to the sappy world of romance? Why can't more men speak the gooey language of love that so many woman long to hear?

Some men, nay, most men are lost when they explore the forests of romantic sentiment. They don't understand why women bawl during movie scenes when the good guy presents the girl with a woolen scarf he wore throughout the Desert Storm war. She had knitted it just for him, and he kept it on his skin twenty-four hours a day during the month of August. The man who watches the movie says, "That was stupid. It's too hot in Iraq to wear a wool scarf!" The woman says, "You don't understand. It's so romantic."

Men would do well to learn the nuances of romantic expression. It's an often-overlooked aspect of chivalry. No, I'm not asking us to feminize ourselves. A man actually has a positive role in romance. He is the brave and gallant hero who, even during horrible torture, thinks of his beloved and his return to her arms. A woman wants to know that she holds a special place in her man's heart, no matter what the circumstances may be.

Romance in all its manifestations boils down to a simple formula. It's the man indicating through his actions "I am thinking about you" even when his woman is not present. It means the man carries her image in his mind even during times of chaos. He detects her scent in the ocean breezes while meditating on a distant shore. He calls out her name during the midnight hour while tossing restlessly because he can't hear her gentle breathing at his side.

Chivalry says, "I value you," using a variety of methods to demonstrate that fact. Acts of romance are simply a sub-set of chivalry. Romantic deeds say, "I value you enough to think about you, even when you're far away, even when my mind is filled with the worries of this world. You are so important to me, not an hour goes by that I don't long to be in your arms. When all is said and done, it is for you that I draw my sword."

Myriad books have been written that give practical advice on how to stoke the flames of romance, and I recommend that the romantically challenged peruse a few. The bottom line, however, in all romantic gestures is to show our wives in tangible ways that we're thinking about them. How can you do this? Surprise your wife with tickets to the theatre, present a room key for a fancy resort, buy her birthstone while you're away on a business trip and wrap it in matching tissue (not toilet paper), send her an e-mail with a photograph of the pillow you have to clutch in her absence. Be creative. Be clever. But most of all, be tangible. Present something physical she can see with her eyes or touch with her hands, something in which you have invested time, energy, or effort to obtain or maintain.

Whether through romance, spiritual leadership, manly protection, or simply not being stupid, chivalry can live again. As we nurture our masculine gentility, we can renew this manly virtue and reestablish it as an expected way of life. Men will be men, and women will be women. Now that's a formula for romance I can relate to.

10

Indivisible and Unconquerable
Once Cleaved, There Is No Cleaving

What God Has Joined Together

I will follow You, Lord," a potential disciple once said to Jesus, "but first permit me to say good-bye to those at home."

Jesus replied, "No one, after putting his hand to the plow and looking back, is fit for the kingdom of God" (see Luke 9:61).

If Jesus walked into your room and said, "Come with me," would you say, "I'll be with you in a minute. I want to finish my sandwich first"? Or "I have this great deal cooking, and it'll be finalized tomorrow"? If He asked you to come with Him, would you even bother to say, "Why?"

Of course not! You would drop everything and jump up to follow Him, a broad smile covering your face as you shiver with excitement that Christ Himself has asked you to do something for Him! What a shame that the vast majority of churchgoers has missed the joy of such unfettered

147

obedience. Although many claim that they would jump up and follow Him, they seem hesitant to submit to the commands Jesus has already revealed in His written Word. Like the man in the Luke 9:57–62 account they say, "I will follow, but allow me to . . ." and they add whatever desire they have that counters what Christ has commanded.

When Jesus walked the earth, He made it clear that such hesitancy to obey is unacceptable. He stated His displeasure in no uncertain terms, saying to those who display lukewarm faithfulness, "I will spit you out of my mouth" (Rev. 3:16). In contrast, some professing Christians today imagine Jesus lovingly patting their selfish heads and crooning, "Of course you may do whatever you wish, precious lambs. Whatever makes you happy. I'll just sit over here and watch you play."

Why do I bring this up, O knight with the shining armor? Because you're a man who is called to ride against the tide. You're a man who is willing to stand against forces that would disgrace the fair name of Jesus. And in order for you to fulfill this noble calling, it's essential that you recognize and understand the most obvious sign of the self-pleasing faith of semi-Christians: divorce.[1]

---

1. At this point, I take great risk. Many of you have already gone through a divorce or have good friends who are divorced. They claim to be Christians, and here I am questioning the authenticity of someone's faith simply because of a "poor decision" he or she has made. If you're an innocent spouse, the victim of divorce who hasn't broken faith, then I'm not talking about you. May God bless your efforts to serve Him in your singleness. For those who have tossed their vows aside, however, I cannot change what the Scripture says, and how you deal with the fact that God hates divorce will be between you and Him. I hope all readers will proceed without offense and learn how to avoid this tragic decision.

Time Out for a Soapbox Sermon

Get ready, guys, because this is one of my hot buttons. When the subject turns to men and women abandoning their vows, their sacred commission to illustrate the union of Christ and His church, I burn with passion. You'd better put on your asbestos-coated reading glasses because this could get rough. I'll get to the funny stuff later.

This deadly, cancerous disease of depraved, selfish minds called divorce is a blight on the church, a sickening stain that spreads its corrupting, lethal venom with every passing year. This corruption is graffiti on our walls that says, "Ha! You're no different, you bunch of hypocrites!" We preach "good news," yet we live in laughable turmoil, ravaged by the very illness we claim to cure.

Have couples completely forgotten these holy vows: "For better or for worse, for richer for poorer, in sickness and in health, 'til death do us part"? With words like these binding two into one inseparable union, a reasonable person would think the divorce rate might be one in a thousand, perhaps one in ten thousand, and with drastically lower percentages in the church.

Rather, the truth about the divorce rate is beyond tragic. With the national rate hovering at around 43 percent of unions,[2] and around 50 percent for couples under the age of 45, the prospect of marriage looks more like a coin flip than a promised life of fidelity. And an even more alarming conclusion comes from the Barna Research Group: "Christians are more likely to experience divorce than are

---

2. Bramlett, Matthew and William Mosher. "First marriage dissolution, divorce, and remarriage: United States," *Advance Data From Vital and Health Statistics*, No. 323. Hyattsville, MD: National Center for Health Statistics: 2001.

non-Christians."[3] Divorce rates are actually higher among professing Christians than among atheists![4]

Such a finding is a tragic slap in the face of Christ, who said,

> Have you not read, that He who created them from the beginning made them male and female, and said, "For this cause a man shall leave his father and mother, and shall cleave to his wife; and the two shall become one flesh"? Consequently they are no longer two, but one flesh. What therefore God has joined together, let no man separate" (Matt. 19:4–6).

God hates divorce (see Mal. 2:16). Trying to deny this fact is like closing our eyes in a hurricane while denying the reality of wind and rain furiously slapping our faces. Yet people make excuses in droves, thinking that their vows are mere ceremony, empty words designed to decorate a beautiful show. It's as though they crossed their fingers while promising marital faithfulness. They believe that somehow God will excuse their mistaken belief that this person was really "The One" whenever they decide the sparkle is gone.

In reality, God has left us with no option; we are to fulfill our vows.

> When you make a vow to the LORD your God, you shall not delay to pay it, for it would be sin in you, and the

---

3. Barna Research Group, 1999-DEC-21. Of course the researchers are not responsible for deciding who is and who is not a true Christian. Their results are based on how the respondents identified themselves.

4. Among atheists the percentage of adults who have been divorced is 21 percent (Barna Research), lower than most religious groups. This statistic doesn't account for the fact that many atheists disdain marriage and choose to cohabit rather than marry. Those who split up after cohabitation are not counted among the divorced, skewing the statistic.

LORD your God will surely require it of you. However, if you refrain from vowing, it would not be sin in you. You shall be careful to perform what goes out from your lips, just as you have voluntarily vowed to the LORD your God, what you have promised (Deut. 23:21–23).

Remember, as this passage noted, we didn't have to make the marriage vow. We could have remained unmarried. We freely decided to speak those words, and we bound ourselves in a sacred covenant. We don't have the option to say, "I didn't know what the future might hold. How could I know things would get so bad?" We promised, "For better or for worse." We said in front of God and man, "Until death do us part." Even if we didn't utter these exact words, we did make a vow of lifelong fidelity and commitment, otherwise it wasn't a marriage at all.

Why do "Christians" divorce at a higher rate than non-Christians? There are two major reasons. The first is simple. Too many people view God as a doting grandfather who just wants to make them happy. I have heard people say, "God wouldn't want me to stay in an unhappy marriage. That's why I knew He wanted me to get a divorce." Seeking only their own pleasure, these people assume that God always blesses their pursuit of happiness. They have molded God into their image, fashioning a bobble-head idol that simply nods "yes" to every whim of its human creator. They are merely playing Christianity, not really walking the bloodstained steps to Calvary. They are like straw houses built on sand. While they close their eyes to the truth, the hurricane strikes, and they are left desolate. Their houses crumble, all because they have denied the reality of the wind and rain, the reality that God really does require their sacrificial allegiance and doesn't condone fleshly indulgence for the sake of "happiness."

What is happiness,[5] anyway? Where does it originate? Was Paul happy when authorities unjustly sent him to prison? As a matter of fact, he was! Singing hymns of praise to God, he celebrated God's goodness even during terrible circumstances (see Acts 16:25). Did the apostles find joy in being flogged? Surprise! They actually enjoyed it! Although the beating itself likely drew moans of agony and painted dark bruises on their aching bodies, they still rejoiced in their suffering (see Acts 5:41).

For a Christian, true happiness comes in pleasing God, especially during great trials. This is the happiness our Lord calls us to seek. God isn't interested in fulfilling our fleshly desires, allowing us to please ourselves in violation of His principles. If Paul had bought into the rationalizations of many today, he might have stayed at home and skipped his missionary journeys. "Traveling is just too hard!" he might have said. "They threw big rocks at me last time. And I can't risk going to places where they'll throw me in jail. I wouldn't be happy there, so God can't be calling me to do that."

Some of Paul's friends did try to prevent him from going to Jerusalem, desiring to keep him out of prison, but he said, "What are you doing, weeping and breaking my heart? For I am ready not only to be bound, but even to die at Jerusalem for the name of the Lord Jesus" (Acts 21:13). This apostle, sold out to the gospel of Christ, had no concern for his bodily pleasure as long as he traveled the road upon which God had called him to suffer.

If Jesus had lived a "please-the-flesh" mentality, He wouldn't have gone to the cross. He might have said, "Father,

---

5. I do not subscribe to the belief that there is a significant difference between "happiness" and "joy." The words are used as practical synonyms in many contexts. Note their parallel use in James 1:2 and 1:12.

you wouldn't ask Me to bleed and die for a bunch of sinners, would You? That wouldn't make Me happy." And He would have skulked out of the garden and avoided the approaching soldiers.

The true story should blare in our minds like a trumpet call to sacrifice. Although Jesus had a bodily desire for the cup of death to pass from His lips, what did He say to His heavenly Father? "Yet not My will, but Thine be done" (Luke 22:42). Going to the cross brought Him true joy, as the Scripture reveals, "Jesus, the author and perfecter of faith, who for the joy set before Him endured the cross, despising the shame, and has sat down at the right hand of the throne of God" (Heb. 12:2). Jesus said to His Father, "I have come . . . to do Thy will" (Heb. 10:7), and this shout of complete obedience echoes in the soul of every true Christian around the world.

What made Jesus "happy"? Pleasing God. What makes Christians happy? The same self-sacrificial search for holiness, the seeking of God's kingdom and His righteousness. Whoever seeks fleshly desires over God's purposes is not a real Christian. "For if you are living according to the flesh, you must die; but if by the Spirit you are putting to death the deeds of the body, you will live. For all who are being led by the Spirit of God, these are sons of God" (Rom. 8:13, 14).

Yes, God wants us to be happy, but of far more importance, God wants us to be holy.[6] On this truth, we can all firmly

---

6. This is not an empty proclamation. I'm not the first to use the happy/holy alliteration, but I know of others who have used it, yet they seem to deny the possibility of complete obedience to God, as though God isn't powerful enough to endow us with His abiding, sanctifying strength. True holiness is possible, and on this solid ground I take my stand.

stand, because as we live holy lives we find true happiness in obedience. This is our joy, to find favor in the eyes of God.

Another reason the divorce rate is so high among "Christians" is that so many of them have bought into the popular "blind-God" concept. They've been taught that sin is normal and that when God looks at them He sees only Jesus. Naturally they conclude, "God won't bring judgment for the sin of divorce. He doesn't even see it. He sees only His dear, sweet Son hanging on a cross." It's as though Christians have a cardboard cutout of Christ shielding them from view.

This heresy threatens to tear down the walls of the church. We might as well close the doors and send everyone home. Not only are we *not* separating ourselves from participation in the world's system, these lies concerning our commitment to marriage covenants have made us worse than the world. Our hypocrisy makes us look like clown-faced charlatans, and people just laugh and shake their heads, thinking, *What a bunch of buffoons! This Christianity sideshow just doesn't work.*

Okay, I'll step off my soapbox and come back to earth. Give me a second to towel off. Whew! After working up a lather over my pet peeve, I'm ready to tackle some nitty-gritty issues.

But What about the Problems?

I know that many people are in desperately horrible marriages, and some endure terrible physical and mental abuse. Yet too many people resort to disobedience, breaking their vows when other solutions are available. My purpose is not to list all the problems and how to address them; dozens of marriage books have already done that. I want to impress upon every reader, however, the absolute necessity and the grave importance of keeping the most sacred of promises. Is any problem too difficult for God to solve? Is there really any reason to seek divorce when we can opt to physically separate temporarily for the sake of sanity or protection? Divorce terminates what God has joined together. It allows man and woman to put a union asunder and defy Jesus, who specifically prohibited such an act. Divorce tells the world that the union between Christ and His church is separable, tenuous, always trembling because of circumstances God could not foresee or forestall.

Since this book is designed to help knights restore or maintain their shining armor, I'll focus my advice on what we men can do to keep our wives from entertaining the specter of divorce. If we do our part and exhibit the unselfish sacrificial life of Christ—the husband of the church—we'll give our wives no reason to seek an escape. Of course, a wife may seek divorce even without a good reason, but we can make sure her excuse doesn't rightfully originate in us.

Pressure Points

Life is like a steam boiler. Daily demands stoke the fire, steam is generated, and pressure builds until we finish each burning task. If demands pile up, and there's no blow-off valve to provide release, only one result is possible. In case you're not familiar with Boyle's and Charles' gas laws and the effects of temperature and pressure changes, I'll put this in layman's terms: "Thar she blows!"

Our busy wives live with pressure every day, and if we're smart we'll do all we can to provide release valves or reduce demands on their time. Otherwise, if pressure persists, our wives might feel the only possible relief lies in changing circumstances, or even the whole environment that has brought them pressure and pain.

I remember when my firstborn child was at a particularly "challenging" stage of development. My wife, Susie, called me at work and said in slow, stress-filled words, "If you don't come home right now, you won't have a son by the end of the day." Even in my youthful ignorance, I could surmise in great understatement, "Well, I suppose something is wrong."

I hurried home, and Susie met me at the front door. She pushed my wiggling son into my arms, snatched my car keys, and ran to the car. "I'll be back," she called through her tears, and then added, "Maybe."

I was stunned. Had I been so blind to the building pressure? Apparently. She did return, feeling much better after blowing off steam. But I learned my lesson. Ever since that day, I've carefully watched for warning signs of impending eruption, and I've looked for ways to provide relief. Here's one that has worked well for our family and became a tradition when our kids were younger. Each Tuesday evening, Susie would take books or magazines to a back room in our house. The children and I would all say that she had gone to Planet X, a faraway celestial body that had no known forms of communication. "Mommy's not really in deep space," I would tell the kids, "but I want you to pretend she is. Bring all your questions to me." I resolved that no crisis could possibly be large enough to pull her back to earth. I'm not quite sure what she did on those evenings, but when the kids were all down for the night she would finally emerge, refreshed and smiling.

Knight, carefully guard your wife's mental well-being. Her life is a never-ending pressure cooker, and it's up to you to find ways to locate her release valves. Give her time alone, take the kids out shopping,[7] or encourage her to go to the library or out with a friend. If you're childless or have older children, go for long walks together and let her vent, or suggest that she go out alone while you cook dinner. This release valve will provide a satisfying flow, and your wife will learn to look to you as a model of Christ, her ultimate sanity saver.

Money, Honey

Financial difficulties often lead to alienation between husbands and wives. Many books have documented the reasons for, and solutions to, money troubles, so I won't dig into that well-mined quarry. Rather, let's focus on what we husbands can do to forestall or mend rifts in our wedded oneness with our wives should the ghosts of dollar signs begin to haunt our homes.

First, as husbands, we need to take our role as providers seriously.[8] We're conduits of God's blessings, channels into which God pours our families' supply. We can't sit at home and collect welfare checks, expecting taxpayers to fund our fattening fannies, or remain in low-paying jobs because we're too lazy to seek higher education or training. Our armor will rust and our minds will turn to mush. Diligence, on the other hand, is a sign of godliness. As we pursue and keep employment that will supply our families with what they need, our wives will trust in our providing ways.

---

7. No, not for ten minutes. A good release requires at least two hours. Four is better. A whole day is ideal.

8. For a more complete essay on this topic, see my book *The Image of a Father*, Chapter 2, "The Father as Provider," AMG Publishers, Chattanooga, 2004.

Second, we need to become unified with our wives concerning family finances, working together as stewards of God's abundant flow. If both spouses in a family earn income, the money should be pooled, avoiding a "my money" and "your money" setup. It's all "God's money," graciously lent to our families to use wisely. Each couple should use their money together, lest they become divided by its power to buy or its power to bring debt.

Susie and I have agreed to make no costly buying decisions without consulting each other. We carefully weigh the benefits of each proposed costly purchase in light of our current supply of money. Whereas we routinely buy such necessities of life as food, medicine, and practical clothing, and trust in God to provide for these essentials, we scrutinize every "luxury" together. That way no huge surprises could tear the financial fabric of our wedded bliss.

Third, as families we need to make a vow of potential poverty. In other words, we should ask ourselves these simple questions: "What would we do if we lose income and have only the bare necessities? Is our love based on riches, or are our hearts united in faith that God is our Lord and will meet our needs? Do we kneel at the altar of material possessions?" Houses fall into ruin, cars rust away, and designer clothes fade into laughable fads, but our vows to stay together, for better or for worse, will last forever. No matter what happens, we and our wives need to pledge to one another that we will be content with what God provides.

As the apostle Paul wrote, "I have learned to be content in whatever circumstances I am. I know how to get along with humble means, and I also know how to live in prosperity; in any and every circumstance I have learned the secret of being filled and going hungry, both of having abundance and suffering need. I can do all things through Him who strengthens me" (Phil. 4:11–13).

One of the best ways to show our faith in God's provision is to give money to those in need. Such an act says, "I freely give, knowing that God will supply." After the paycheck hits the bank, what's the first check we write? If it goes toward someone else's needs, we make a statement of faith, in concert with our wives, and our vow of potential poverty is sealed in concrete reality. In other words, our only assurance that we'll have enough in our pantries stems from the promises of God. If the pantry lacks the finer foods in life, we'll have the opportunity to practice contentment, making our resolve stronger should more trying times come our way.

Money is a tool, a powerful possession we can use for good or evil. Beware of its dark side. Money masquerades as a provider, its power to deliver goods making it look like the source of bountiful supply. It can be an idol, and millions of people flock to its altar of worship. If money leaves a home through unemployment or injury, its worshippers often fret and their faith is dashed. But if we look past money's green façade to the true Lord of all, we maintain our confidence, knowing that the God of the universe, the supplier of all that is good, never fails to provide for His obedient people.

Knights, don't let money come between you and your wives. Financial pressures can try to slice away at your precious union, but when you tackle the problems together, with full assurance in God's provision, you can face them as a team.

Skin-deep: Wrinkles, Liver Spots, and Other Wonders of Aging

Believe it or not, we're getting older. In fact, in all likelihood we'll also get quite ugly, at least according to popular definitions of beauty. We can slow the process by trying to outrun wrinkles and spray away the gray, but we can't change the ultimate truth of mortality. We're going to get old and die.

Many men are attracted to their ladies because of their outer beauty. What a surprise! Guys enjoy looking at what God designed especially for them, the wonderful female form. Unfortunately, this feature is often the deciding factor, and a man may overlook the more unattractive, inner traits of his chosen woman in order to get the prettiest one.

Of course, there's nothing wrong with us wanting our wives to be physically attractive. If they take care of their bodies and maintain cleanliness, they are showing signs of discipline that likely extend to other areas. But the proof, as one of my favorite food clichés says, is in the pudding. Eye-popping looks aren't going to last, for us or for our wives, so we'd better nurture our wives' inner qualities and learn to appreciate them more than the smooth curves.

So, knight, pursue your wife's heart and learn to love it. Help it to blossom into brilliant colors of love and faithfulness. If you adore her inner self, you'll never lament the decay of her outer form, the flower of youth that once graced God's garden. Lumps and scales will replace silky skin, and curves will reshape into twisted frames, yet you'll still find her lovely as your hands caress her outer, wilting petals. Her frail body may lie paralyzed someday in a bed of lost hope, and still you'll lovingly cultivate her failing self-confidence as you speak of her germinating love, a love that springs forth as flowers of praise to God in gardens all over the world. Her inner beauty has spread the seeds of the gospel in messages of faith and holiness everywhere her feet have trod.

And we, O knights of the balding head and widening girth, will also fade into less-than-perfect models of godlike physique. Yes, we should exercise and try to maintain excellent physical health, but we should concentrate even more on cultivating our inner attractiveness, which is like a garden that never dies. We must pursue such qualities as wisdom, kindness, humility, and contentment, which will guarantee our wives' satisfaction with our presence as we grow old together.

One day Geritol® will replace milk in your cereal, and bran flakes will arrive at your home in thirty-gallon drums. You'll brush your teeth with both hands, the brush in one hand and your teeth in the other. The creaking sounds at night will be your joints, and instead of cologne, the aroma of Bengay® will drift through your bedroom. An exciting night on the town will include going to the grocery store to try to redeem a handful of expired coupons and then to the Wal-Mart to buy a pair of black socks to go with your khaki shorts and tennis shoes. Glasses may grow thicker than a stack of nickels, and you might search the whole house for them even though they're sitting on your forehead.

Although our bodies fall apart, if we pursue inner strength our armor will shine ever brighter. Instead of just becoming ugly old men, we'll become beautiful servants of God who happen to be living in decaying bodies. This is all godly women ever really want, anyway.

Growing Old Together

Our hair grows thin in graying strands;
Our lips aren't ruby red.
Our bodies curve in places where
The young would surely dread.

Our skin is rough and cracking dry;
Our eyes a bloodshot hue.
Our socks now weigh a dozen pounds
And squeeze our veins so blue.

Our vision blurs so when we cook,
We stir in God knows what,
And leave it burning on the stove
Till sludge forms in the pot.

Our dinner tastes like motor oil
And stinks of something worse.
So losing taste and sense of smell
Is blessing, not a curse.

We pace the house, go to and fro,
Determined, yet insane,
For when we enter any room,
We wonder why we came!

Yes, we're old and feeble now;
Our eyes have lost their glow.
Our muscles shrink and fade away,
While ears and nose still grow.

Yet still you say, "I love you so"
And I still love you, too.
Though bodies crumble, minds grow dull,
Our spirits yet renew.

And wrapped in warm and tender arms,
I feel your vow to cleave.
Though knees and elbows bend and crack,
I know you'd never leave.

What foolish thoughts! A mindless jest!
My faithful wife, I tease,
For even if you sought to go,
You'd never find the keys!

—BRYAN DAVIS

A Final Word on Faithfulness

There are many other forces that try to tear married couples apart: family pressures, spiritual persecution, and mental illness, just to name a few. Every one, however, is anticipated in this wedding vow: "for better or for worse." God still commands us to keep our unions whole. Only adultery remains as the true break in the marriage covenant, and even then we're not commanded to divorce. God still hates divorce, although He allows it when sexual unfaithfulness destroys the bond. Even when it is allowed, though, divorce still stains the beautiful image of Christ and the church. Divorce, even because of adultery, stands as a symbol of failure, a precious pearl intentionally thrown into a sewer for the sake of a few minutes of pleasure by the adulterer or adulteress.

Men, if we ever forsake our vows of fidelity, we'll not only destroy our sacred bond with our wives, but we'll also prove our unfaithfulness to God. The Bible says, "Or do you not know that the unrighteous shall not inherit the kingdom of God? Do not be deceived; neither fornicators, nor idolaters, nor adulterers, nor effeminate, nor homosexuals, nor thieves, nor the covetous, nor drunkards, nor revilers, nor swindlers, shall inherit the kingdom of God" (1 Cor. 6:9, 10). Don't commit adultery. It's simply not worth it. How could a moment or two of fleshly spasms be worth destroying the sacred covenant of love? How could it be worth an eternity in hell?

My fellow knights, learn to keep your eyes only on your wife. Never let them stray. She is your one and only, and your devotion to her alone is like a pleasing aroma, an earthly portrait of Christ's love. Let your mind and body delight in her. As you continue in wholehearted fidelity, if she's a woman of God she will gladly return your faithfulness and never consider the advances of another man.

11

A Damsel in Distress?
Sorry, I've Retired from the Rescue Business

What is the heart of romance? For many women, it's a dashing young knight rescuing a fair maiden from the clutches of a dangerous ne'er-do-well. She's entranced by his willingness to sacrifice, his strength to overcome the shiftless skunk who had less-than-honorable intentions, and his gallantry so freely given with no thought of reward.

When the spirit of a true knight demonstrates the courage and honor of a gentleman warrior, and exercises gallantry in helping a woman, his efforts may capture her heart. He may attract her attention and affection, even though he's unaware that he has turned her head.

What could be more natural? Kindness in the form of chivalry is attractive, and women tend to take notice. This masculine magnetism probably contributed to your wife's fondness of you. It's an important characteristic of your shining armor, and the gleam of tender compassion is brighter than almost any other luster in your polished surface. If your gallantry attracted your wife, and you are still your wife's hero, you've done well. Keep it up. That aspect of your wedded bliss should never lose its shine.

Beware, however, of letting the gleam of manly aid fall across the eyes of other women. You've entranced one woman—your wife—and that's enough. This rule is sort of like fishing laws. You've reached your limit, so there's no use putting your line or net back into the water to rescue a floundering flounder in the drying shallows. Although she wiggles and gasps for breath, it's not your job to provide personal aid. Get help from a female, and let her minister to this sister in need.

Is this response heartless and cruel? It may seem that way, but any efforts on your part would not only seem fishy to others, you would run the risk of setting a hook[1] in another woman's heart. Why? The hearts of millions of females long for knights to sweep them away, but you're not available.

Lonely Hearts

M any women don't receive tender attention from true men. These women either have no fulfilling relationship with men, or the men in their lives don't know how to demonstrate the gentle, yet strong, leadership of a compassionate warrior. If you, in good conscience, display one-on-one acts of kindness to a woman like this, she may respond in ways you might not expect. Even if your motives are pure, she may view your benevolent act as an invitation, an open door for her to seek further kindnesses. You have stirred up good feelings, and she may long for more even though you are married to someone else.

In cases like these, the most common danger is the unnecessary pain that grows in a love-struck woman who

---

1. This is the last of the fishing metaphors. I promise.

can't morally pursue her dream man—you. Even a godly woman will feel the natural draw, although she will resist its pull. Why risk giving her emotional injury?

A secondary danger also lurks. If the woman chooses to pursue your time and attention, you may feel obligated to continue your courtesies. This woman has no one to lead her out of her troubles, and your natural desire is to keep lending her a guiding hand. In the process, though, her heart may knit to yours, and her increasing attention may cause your affections to wander. If she's attractive, you can feel the excitement of her pursuit. It feeds your ego. And if your wife hasn't been attentive to you physically, this new woman's open warmth may stoke a fire that has been cold for too long. Could the spark of potential adultery be kindled?

The embers of adultery are unable to grow in ashes doused with cold reality. Although a woman may be charmed by your gallant actions and her heart's fire is kindled, you can extinguish any flames of romance by terminating this rescuing relationship. Any man who extends a helping hand to a woman who isn't his wife is playing with fire. Don't strike that match. If you've already lit a flame, douse it immediately. A hungry female's heart is easy to set aflame. Don't get burned.[2] Remember these words: "Can a man take fire in his bosom, and his clothes not be burned? Or can a man walk on hot coals, and his feet not be scorched?" (Prov. 6:27, 28).

You may be certain that you will never fall prey to a woman's pursuit, yet it would still be a mistake to incite her romantic notions. If you hear a damsel's cry of distress, turn to your church's women's ministries group for help. Seek your wife's aid. Do whatever you have to do to bring in another woman's assistance. Even if you have to take

---

2. Okay, that's the last fire metaphor, at least for a while.

immediate action to rescue a damsel in distress, if she seeks further help, ask your pastor to assign a female whom the damsel can call. The help she really needs lies in the heart of a wise woman (see Titus 2:3–5).

When I was newly married, I worked for the Billy Graham Crusade for a while, answering telephones during evenings when Dr. Graham's crusades appeared on television. A hundred phones sat in cubicles in the basement of a church, and their lights flashed constantly, as needy people called for help in response to Dr. Graham's message. Each time I picked up the handset, I had no idea what kind of aid would be required. Would it be for marital counseling? A request for prayer? A suicide call? A lonely heart?

In a moment of mind-boggling ignorance, I made the innocent mistake of offering my home phone number to a desperate, lonely female. She lived in my city, so I thought I might be able to help her. Her voice made her sound like she was about ninety years old. Her crying pleas tugged at my heart. *This poor, needy lady,* I thought, *surely could use ongoing aid.*

What a mistake! She latched onto me like a leech with barbed fingernails, calling me every evening, begging me to stay on the line to ease her pangs of loneliness. I experienced firsthand what power a tender-hearted man can have on a woman, even though the effect wasn't intended. Every time the phone rang, my wife and I stiffened, dreading another hour of repetitive counseling. This daily servitude took its toll on my wife, and I struggled as well. How could I shake this poor lady loose? My mind was caught in the tension between wanting to help and realizing that her selfish demands for my time were hurting my relationship with my true love.

When my ear finally swelled to the size of a watermelon, I told the woman not to call me again, and it took several refusals to answer the phone before she finally got the message. I received permission to give her the phone number of a godly woman at my church, but as far as I know she never contacted her. Apparently she had knit her heart to me, the gallant male she had never previously encountered, and I was too inexperienced to recognize that possibility when I gave her my number.

Men, as hard as it might be, avoid damsels in distress. As our wives see our unwillingness to capture other women's hearts, even by accident, they'll learn to trust us all the more. They'll know that we've set our minds only on them, and that we have no intention of entertaining any notion of attracting other females. To set our wives' minds at ease and solidify our holy vows in deed as well as in word is our sacred duty. Their hearts will never be troubled, and the specter of adultery will forever be banished from their minds.

Skin Cancer?

There is another kind of adulterous woman who lurks in the shadows, quiet and unseen, without consistent shape or physical substance, yet she is more alluring than the street harlot and just as destructive as the motel tryst. She seeks your company, often posing as a damsel in distress. Her poses beg for your attention; she seeks to be rescued from loneliness. Although she wears no clothes, she bears a sword, ready to cut your heart in two, setting body in conflict with spirit. From the slick pages of a magazine or the colorful images of a computer screen, she awaits your peering eyes, ready to strike with her naked dagger. She is the harlot of pornography.

Why do the hearts of so many married men become divided? Although they have wives whom God designed to meet their physical needs, why are they tempted to seek the pleasures of another? For many men, physical adultery is a well-recognized taboo. Physically violating the wedding vows, even in our permissive society, is still considered by most Christians to be a sign of unfaithfulness to God, an act that proves an unsaved spiritual state (see 1 Cor. 6:9). A divided heart that leads to spiritual adultery, however, has not gained such public condemnation. Millions of men dive into the cesspool of pornography, purposely filling their eyes with forbidden fruit. Although they may never touch another woman's body, their minds entertain the thoughts, their lusts traveling from woman to woman, gaining mental and even physical pleasure from the images these willing females produce.

What is the allure of the undressed and apparently sexually insatiable women? With pursed, come-hither lips, she curls her inviting finger, exposing and caressing her smooth, airbrushed flesh. She is the image of desire, a lonely woman begging for a man's fulfilling touch, and not just any man. She wants you. She's begging for you to take her and have your way with her. She's there for your pleasure. "Come and take me," she calls. "I need you!"

And it's all a lie.

The woman is a whore. She poses for money, nothing more, nothing less. She doesn't care about any man who mentally rapes her with his eyes and mind. In fact, if you venture into her lair, she will likely disdain or even hate you, perhaps laughing at your weakness as she overpowers you so easily with a mere flash of flesh. How many men have allowed her to poison their minds, committing spiritual adultery with this harlot of hate who reveals her body while stealing a man's soul?

For the lips of an adulteress drip honey,
And smoother than oil is her speech;
But in the end she is bitter as wormwood,
Sharp as a two-edged sword.
Her feet go down to death,
Her steps lay hold of Sheol.
She does not ponder the path of life;
Her ways are unstable, she does not know it
    (Prov. 5:3–6).

Pornography is a simple formula, although the user allows himself to be unaware of its devices. It invites wandering eyes to drink from its lovely pool, promising a quenched thirst. Alas! The thirst is far from quenched! The harlot's drink is a pill of salt; it makes a man beg for deeper draughts, more skin, younger girls, views of lesbian encounters, until images alone are unable to satisfy. Each sip whets the addiction as a man is entrapped by the harlot's poison, and his mind is imprisoned in pornography's deadly snare. Solomon wrote, "For on account of a harlot one is reduced to a loaf of bread, and an adulteress hunts for the precious life" (Prov. 6:26).

Jesus said, "Everyone who looks on a woman to lust for her has committed adultery with her already in his heart" (Matt. 5:28). Can a man claim that he looks at images of nude women without lusting, that his reasons for seeking the harlot's exposed skin are holy? Hardly! This lust is adultery, pure and simple, and a man who pursues this course has broken his vows. And with whom has he mated? He has pursued a mere phantom. He has thrown away his virtue for colored dots on a printed page. He has cast away his wife in pursuit of pixels on a computer screen.

The Internet has certainly helped pornography purveyors capture a whole host of men. An innocent engine search may yield a dozen lurid descriptions, inviting a simple click to reach images of women who beg for your attention. No magazines to hide. No trips to the video store. No evidence of evil. One mouse click and a dozen smiling beauties await your caressing eyes. Simple curiosity leads many into the snare, trapping the minds of those who don't dash for the exit in disgust. First a sip, then a draught, and the harlot has captured another lover. But where is thy wife, O man! For whom hast thou cast her aside?

> Drink water from your own cistern,
> And fresh water from your own well.
> Should your springs be dispersed abroad,
> Streams of water in the streets?
> Let them be yours alone,
> And not for strangers with you.
> Let your fountain be blessed,
> And rejoice in the wife of your youth.
> As a loving hind and a graceful doe,
> Let her breasts satisfy you at all times;
> Be exhilarated always with her love.
> For why should you, my son, be exhilarated with
> an adulteress,
> And embrace the bosom of a foreigner?
> (Prov. 5:15–20).

Why do so many men seek strange flesh? The mystery of the unknown? The excitement of the forbidden? The desire to conquer? Any of these excuses is surely inadequate. There is simply no good reason, as Proverbs 6:32, 33 reveals:

The one who commits adultery with a woman is lacking
    sense;
He who would destroy himself does it.
Wounds and disgrace he will find,
And his reproach will not be blotted out.

Let's get real, guys. What's this pornography stuff all about, anyway? Freak shows aside, more than 99 percent of the women in these pictures look pretty much alike, with body parts in the same places. Breasts are in front, buttocks are in back, there are two arms and two legs, and an epidermis holds it all together. There aren't many surprise arrangements. There goes the mystery excuse. And we won't conquer these women; they're untouchable. In fact, if we lust after them, they've conquered us. We've fallen into their trap.

That leaves us with the excitement-of-the-forbidden excuse, the hormonal rush that accompanies the peek through the keyhole, the stolen view of what lies beneath the clothing, the places no one is allowed to see. "Come take a look, Mister, and I'll show you something you'll like . . . just for you."

Get over it. These women aren't giving you a private glance; they're strutting their stuff for anyone with eyes. Forbidden? Yes. For your eyes only? Forget about it. These harlots put their bodies on show, inviting more intimate exposure for paying customers. All they really want is your money. You would waste your endorphins on a lie—hate masquerading as love. The hormonal rush prompts the desire for more as each drink creates new thirst.

If you're addicted to pornography, you need to meditate on reality—the truth of the hateful harlot. She's a stalker, a seductress, a destroyer. She will poison your soul. She has nothing to offer that you haven't seen before; even her body is just a fleeting image. She's certainly not a damsel in distress, and it's not your duty to rescue her, even in your mind. Tell me, would you look at pornographic images with your wife? Would you sit down and say, "Honey, come take a look at this gal! Isn't she hot?" May it never be! Such an act would be shameful. Yet this is a good test and a faithful standard to use in avoiding what is shameful. If you're ever contemplating an act, ask yourself if you would do it in your wife's presence. If the answer is no, then don't do it.

Say this along with me: "I will never do anything in private for which I would be ashamed in public." Repeat this promise, and embed it in your mind.

Remember, too, that you're never really in private. God always looks over your shoulder. Would you say to Him, "Get a load of this one, Lord! She's a looker!" God forbid! Yet millions of men act as though God can't see them. But He not only sees everything in your view, but He also reads everything in your mind. He is watching. Do we believe it? Do we care? Will we invite Him to inspect everything we view? Would we mind showing to Jesus Christ everything we bring up on our computer screens, every image our eyes rest upon in magazines, every television channel that makes us pause as we look for a decent program?

Isn't this the test of faith? Isn't how we act in private a true reflection of what we believe about God, that He is really who He says He is, the ever-present, omniscient Lord?

How do I know about pornography and its power? I once dove into that cesspool. Years before I gave my life to Christ, I sought the excitement of the forbidden, the hormonal rush that made my heart beat faster and my teenaged hands shake with anticipation. Thanks be to God, my swim in the sewer was brief. Although I did not yet know Him, I believe God helped me discern the folly of allowing these images to control my mind.

To this day, I regret that plunge into evil. Some of those images haunted my mind for years, stamped into my memory like a searing brand. Such is the power of a pornographic image. The chemical high makes it adhere to the mind. The memories fly like bats unbidden and lurk during both waking and sleeping moments.

Yet there is a cure. As we set our minds on the things above, where Christ is, memories of evil begin to vanish. As Paul taught:

> If then you have been raised up with Christ, keep seeking the things above, where Christ is, seated at the right hand of God. Set your mind on the things above, not on the things that are on earth. For you have died and your life is hidden with Christ in God (Col. 3:1–3).

> Finally, brethren, whatever is true, whatever is honorable, whatever is right, whatever is pure, whatever is lovely, whatever is of good repute, if there is any excellence and if anything worthy of praise, let your mind dwell on these things. The things you have learned and received and heard and seen in me, practice these things; and the God of peace shall be with you (Phil. 4:8, 9).

Even if you have imbibed the poison of pornography for years, God can give you peace. Give your life to Christ, and He will shatter the unfruitful images as your mind learns to dwell on what is pure and honorable. Leave your adulterous ways behind, and God will help you walk in holiness, giving you the ability never to stray again in your mind.

Your wife is your one and only damsel. Never seek another. Let her breasts satisfy you at all times, and be exhilarated always with her love.

12

Passing on the Legacy
Like Father, Like Son

The old man pushed his wheelchair toward the arm of the recliner and grabbed the remote control. With an emphatic click he silenced the television and tossed the remote toward the teenager lounging on the chair.

The boy jerked up and caught the remote in both hands. "Hey, Grandpa, what gives? I thought you like D-day movies."

Grandpa nodded. "I do, Michael . . . I do, but I think it's time we had a little talk."

Michael sat up straight and smiled. "A talk? You mean another war story?"

Grandpa pulled off his thick glasses and shakily wiped his upper lip with a handkerchief. "Yes, I have a war story to tell, but it's a new one."

"I don't mind the old ones, especially when they're about you storming the beach at Normandy."

Grandpa waved his hand. "No, not that kind of story. I want to tell a war story about your father."

"Dad? He was never in a war." Michael rolled his eyes. "Bookkeepers over at Ace Plastics just shoot numbers back and forth. Dad probably wouldn't even know how to hold a gun."

"That's what you think." Grandpa sighed and shook his head. His sigh ended in a whisper. "If only you knew."

Michael's brow furrowed, and he leaned forward, lowering his voice. "Only knew what?"

Grandpa pushed his wheelchair closer. "Remember when you were no bigger than your sister? I used to tell you stories about knights in shining armor and how they fought dragons and rescued fair maidens."

"Yeah. I still remember some of them. I always pictured you as the knight."

Grandpa lowered his head and nodded. "Well, I always pictured your father as the knight, and that's who I wanted you to see in those stories."

"Dad as a knight? No way! I mean, Dad's a nice guy and everything, but you're the one who lost a leg on D-day. You're the one who rescued six guys in your platoon and personally took out a machine-gun nest."

Grandpa's face turned gray, and a tear formed in one eye. "Yeah, all that stuff's true, but I'm also the guy who got thrown out of the house by your grandmother, the guy who couldn't keep his other two sons out of jail, and the guy who couldn't keep his daughter from running off with free-love hippies in the sixties."

Michael stayed quiet for a few seconds, staring at his grandfather in disbelief. "You . . . you never told me about those things."

Grandpa shook his head slowly. "And neither did your father. He would never tell you bad things about me or your aunt and uncles."

"Dad doesn't really talk much about anybody, except for Mom . . . and God."

Grandpa extended his finger and thrust it toward Michael. "Exactly! That's why he's the one you should be looking up to, not me. Even though I didn't raise him right, he still turned out to be the knight in the stories I told you when you were little." Grandpa waved his hand at the television. "It's one thing to be brave when you're storming the beach to keep the world safe from tyrants, but sometimes it's just as brave to be faithful to your wife and children, to show them love every single day without messing up like I did." He pointed toward a family portrait near the windowsill. "I think it's easier to rush into a hail of bullets for one day than it is to sacrifice your own desires for thousands of days like your father has. I learned that lesson a little too late."

"Sacrifice? What does Dad sacrifice?"

Grandpa snorted. "What *doesn't* he sacrifice? He goes to a tiresome job every day for a boss who only cares about money. He visits your church's mission church in Haiti every two years—visits, by the way, that you always refuse to go on, because they'd be 'too boring.' And, to top it off, I'll bet he never told you he was a guitar-playing musician. When you came along he didn't want to be away from home so much, so he gave up the traveling and learned bookkeeping." Grandpa reached over and put a tender hand on Michael's shoulder. "Your father gave up something he loved because he wanted to be with someone he loved even more."

Michael stared into his grandfather's sad old eyes and watched a tear slowly slide down his cheek. He couldn't say anything. He just nodded.

Grandpa took his handkerchief and wiped his face before wheeling his chair toward the hallway. He stopped and looked back. "I guess that's the end of my story. Knights in shining armor don't always have swords you can see. I hope you won't forget that."

Michael watched the old man roll away. He sniffed back his own tears and whispered, "No . . . I won't forget it."

Pass It On

How do we pass on the lessons of "The Old Code," the legacy of the knight in shining armor? Many of you reading this book have sons or daughters who need to witness the example of the shining knight and hear his voice spelling out principles of manly discipline. You need to know how to communicate the heart and soul of your message, using words that reflect the inner purity of a man of valor. Simply put, you need to fearlessly tell the truth of the wondrous work God is doing in you to make you a godly man fashioned after His own heart.

Even if you aren't a father, you can still pass on the great truths of godly masculinity. A generation of youth is searching for spiritual champions who will stand as beacons of virtue. These young people watch your actions—how you act with your spouse, how you defend her body and mind, and how you carry out selfless acts of chivalry. They examine your day-to-day activities to see if your walk matches your talk.

Our culture offers few models of gallant male warriors. In fact, as we noted earlier, it typically serves up the opposite, putting men on display who are like clueless buffoons or sex-crazed monkeys. We, on the other hand, are commissioned to teach another standard—one that exemplifies men who bridge the enormous gap between God's ideals and those of our virtually neutered male population. We are to be models for a generation that knows nothing about the Old Code, the holy standards that bring about the rebirth of an endangered species—the strong, courageous, gentleman warrior.

But where can our sons find guidance? To whom should they look to find men to emulate, mentors espousing the masculine? Our sons—young men at church, male acquaintances with whom we share offices, guys we meet at athletic courts and backyard barbecues—need our model of gallantry. These men need to see examples of people who ooze the contagious qualities of chivalrous conquerors and shine with the pristine polish that only knights in shining armor can reflect.

Just as our sons need guidance and a standard, so do our daughters. With hearts aching to meet earthly models of Jesus Christ, our daughters long for real men—not the spineless pretenders on prime-time television or the promise-breaking charlatans in politics or the rebellious, hippie retros of the modern music and art cultures. These girls and young women need men who blaze with the glorious flame of Christ, lighting a lady's path and leading the way in this dark, sin-sick world.

Without knowing what a man ought to be, our daughters may latch onto lesser men of this world, unaware that God is preparing true gentlemen. Without the witness of our living examples, young ladies may never realize that such godly men exist.

Even though a man may cheat, lie, and commit unfaithful acts, a young woman might still settle for such a low-life character, sighing in resignation to herself, *Oh, well, that's just what men are like.* This isn't a stretch. How many times have you heard women complain, "All men are alike" or "All men are after just one thing." With the predominance of sexual perverts who interpret a casual smile as an invitation to the bedroom, or weak-minded fools who can't think without a parallel sports metaphor, or spiritual illiterates who don't know the difference between the Old Testament and the New Testament, is it any wonder that women think this way?

We can change this catastrophic worldview. We can help our sons and daughters learn a new paradigm that really isn't

new—the Old Code, the culturally forsaken ways of righteous men. As men, husbands, and fathers, we are to teach
the next generations. As the psalmist wrote in Psalm 78:1–8:

> Listen, O my people, to my instruction;
> Incline your ears to the words of my mouth.
> I will open my mouth in a parable;
> I will utter dark sayings of old,
> Which we have heard and known,
> And our fathers have told us.
> We will not conceal them from their children,
> But tell to the generation to come the praises of the
>   LORD,
> And His strength and His wondrous works that He
>   has done.
> For He established a testimony in Jacob,
> And appointed a law in Israel,
> Which He commanded our fathers,
> That they should teach them to their children,
> That the generation to come might know, even the
>   children yet to be born,
> That they may arise and tell them to their children,
> That they should put their confidence in God,
> And not forget the works of God,
> But keep His commandments,
> And not be like their fathers,
> A stubborn and rebellious generation,
> A generation that did not prepare its heart,
> And whose spirit was not faithful to God.

Our examples of proper manhood are our most important teaching tools. How we treat our wives shines as the
brightest light in our children's practical guidance curricula.
How we live in day-to-day obedience to God fills out the

story of our hearts, the inner holiness that makes us imitators of Christ.

We need, however, to relate these Bible-based, Old Code truths in a systematic fashion, giving our children a reason to believe while providing a standard for reference. In other words, we are called to help them understand why we act the way we do. Christian men who walk in true integrity are the oddballs of our culture.

- When personally attacked, we turn the other cheek.
- When maligned, we pray for our enemies.
- When cursed, we offer a blessing.
- We help old ladies cross the street and turn our eyes away from scantily clad females.
- We study the Word of God, giving the pages of Scripture more time than we give the sports section of the newspaper.
- We stay on our knees longer than we sit idly on the sofa.

Armed with God-given strength—physical, spiritual, mental, and emotional—we're ready to charge into the fray for the sake of others. With our muscles rippling and our voices raising a battle cry, we bear swords of virtue sharpened for godly warfare. We are the odd ones, holy men of sacrifice in a society of self-seeking males.

Sadly, many churches have failed to teach the godly standard of the virtuous warrior. So, the only way to explain our chivalry to a new generation is to paint a clear portrait of a man of God who is unashamed of the holy standard—the pattern of righteousness in Christ.

In painting that picture, I'll revisit a few issues I mentioned in earlier chapters. This is the most important lesson in the entire book, so we're going to get serious again. Stay close and read with spiritual eyes. The story I'll tell isn't popular in some Christian circles, but it describes the ever-lasting song of God's holy provision, what it means to be a true man of God.

A Herald of Holiness

Why is the Old Code called "Old"? What caused it to fade into the shadows? What made its shining armor rust and fall into disuse, finally to be ignored by generations who wouldn't recognize its worth? The simple answer is our culture's rejection of holiness.

There was a day when obedience to God wasn't a tired cliché; it was living, breathing Christianity. Moses was read in our churches, and we heard passages like this one:

> Hear, O Israel! The LORD is our God, the LORD is one! And you shall love the LORD your God with all your heart and with all your soul and with all your might. And these words, which I am commanding you today, shall be on your heart; and you shall teach them diligently to your sons and shall talk of them when you sit in your house and when you walk by the way and when you lie down and when you rise up. And you shall bind them as a sign on your hand and they shall be as frontals on your forehead. And you shall write them on the doorposts of your house and on your gates (Deut. 6:4–9).

Then we all said "Amen" with our voices and in our hearts, knowing that the commandment was not too diffi-cult to obey (see Deut. 30:11). When we listened to the words of Jesus, "If you abide in My word, then you are truly disciples of Mine; and you shall know the truth, and the truth shall make you free" (John 8:31, 32), we trusted these as the very words of God, knowing that any sin was a sign of spiritual slavery. As Jesus said, "Truly, truly, I say to you, everyone who commits sin is the slave of sin" (John 8:34).

What has changed? To whom was Jesus referring when He said these words to His disciples?

"You are the light of the world. A city set on a hill cannot be hidden. Nor do men light a lamp, and put it under the peck-measure, but on the lampstand; and it gives light to all who are in the house. Let your light shine before men in such a way that they may see your good works, and glorify your Father who is in heaven" (Matt. 5:14–16).

Are we lights of the world? Are we beacons for our culture? Do we shine the truth of God's word from a position that cannot be reproached, or do we allow darkness to flood our lives? If we really believe that God's Spirit can give us victory, then we have every reason to have confidence in our ability to obey His word and live as models of holy conduct.

As God's men we must believe that God's promises are true, that we really can be like Christ. Those who love God are actually predestined to be like the Son of God (see Rom. 8:29). Therefore, we can be the men God has called us to be. Jesus wasn't joking when He said, "If anyone wishes to come after Me, let him deny himself, and take up his cross, and follow Me" (Matt. 16:24). If these words of Scripture don't speak truth to us, then we might as well pack up our false bravado, throw our swords back into our closets, and join the ranks of the self-absorbed. If we can't really become like Christ, then trying to follow Him is a hopeless crusade. We're just chasing false visions.

But we're promised victory! We can be holy men of God. What did Paul say? "Be imitators of me, just as I also am of Christ" (1 Cor. 11:1). Paul believed in his ability to follow his master, and he called us to the same standard. He was ready to be a powerful example of Christian manhood, ready to die for the sake of the gospel. He refused to turn aside in fear when called upon to bleed for his crucified Savior.

Once we understand the reality of our position in Christ—being dead to sin and alive to God (see Rom. 6:11)—we'll not only live this kind of obedient life, we'll be able to teach it with authority, becoming heralds of holiness for future generations.

Practically speaking, this means that our words should always reflect our confidence in God's power in our lives. We should not allow our culture's downward spiral capture our confidence in Christ and drag us into the moral morass of weak-minded faith. We're strong because Jesus Christ has made us strong. We're holy because we died with Him and were raised up to new life. This is not just a theoretical position in God's sight, but a real, flesh-and-blood, day-to-day existence. Since our righteous Shepherd blazed this holy path and set it before us, we should have confidence that we will be able to follow in His footsteps.

A Living Example

Jesus set down a path for us to follow. He created a model of behavior that we can read about and imitate. He knew that His people would need to see their master's footsteps in order to have the faith to follow, so He created a lasting legacy of humble obedience to His heavenly Father.

Our children need the same kind of witness. It isn't enough to preach sermons and point to what might appear to them as faded words in a dusty Bible. Our children need us to stand as physical models of behavior, unafraid of scrutiny as we say to them, "Yes, you can follow me. I won't lead you astray." Young people often respond more readily to an illustration than to an explanation. That's why our examples as living, breathing men of God are crucial. We need to show the next generation what ruling over our body means (see 1 Cor. 9:24–27). We need to model the mental discipline that enables us to accurately handle the word of truth (see 2 Tim. 2:15). We need to emerge in their sight as spiritual lights in the darkness (see Matt. 5:14).

To stay in shape, I try to run at least four times a week. As all runners know, this discipline requires an element of mind over matter. If we want to gain stamina, we have to endure pain and refuse our bodies' request to stop and take a breather. Following the apostle Paul's illustration of an enduring runner, I decided that running a marathon would be a good way to show my children a model of overcoming the desires of the body.

Although the training regimen was torture, I was able to complete the marathon, even though I broke my foot at about the twenty-three mile marker. The stress fracture forced me to push through excruciating spasms for the last three miles. When I arrived at home I elevated my foot on the table to ease the pain. A banana-shaped bruise decorated my skin at the break point, and three blackened toes told the story of the incessant pounding they endured. It was a great illustration of overcoming the flesh, and I believe I gained respect in my children's eyes, even though I wonder if they wavered between considering me brave and questioning my sanity. I trust, in any case, that they will remember this lesson in mastering physical desires.

It's also important to model our mental discipline. My children know that they can ask me any question, no matter how puzzling. Although I'll admit my ignorance on many topics, they know they can count on me to search out the answers. They have watched me study the Word, and they trust me as a reliable source of wisdom as I provide (I hope) insightful responses, adding probing questions of my own to further stimulate their thinking. From academics to religion to politics, we wrestle with the great questions of our time and times past. And the satisfaction my children and I get from exercising our brains creates a bond of trust.

My children also trust me as a spiritual adviser. After listening to years of my Bible teaching and watching how I have applied godly principles in my life, they have gained confidence that I can give them valuable counsel in seeking God's kingdom. Whether we laugh or cry together, they have faith that they can entrust me with their deepest thoughts. Why? Because they have seen me laugh with joy over God's blessings, and they have seen me cry with those who have been wounded by life's traumas. They know that I'll reach out with the hands of mercy that Christ has taught me to bear.

Don't be ashamed to think that you can be a model of Christ. Even if you have failed in the past, any man who really wants to follow Christ will be able to find His footsteps and follow them. And don't fall into the trap of false humility, thinking it arrogant to believe we can answer such a calling. Jesus commanded us to follow Him, and He knows our abilities better than we do. Walk those steps in faith; He'll give you the power you need to follow.

There is no greater joy than to feel the pleasure of our Master, Jesus Christ. As we walk in obedience and, by our example, pass to the next generation the image of His holiness, we are guaranteed to hear His welcoming call, "Come, you who are blessed of My Father, inherit the kingdom prepared for you from the foundation of the world" (Matt. 25:34).

Christat, Our Model

The Old Code need not die if we pass it on. Teach the truth to the next generation. Tell them about Christ, the holy One, your model of manhood. Demonstrate a sacrificial life of leadership for your wife, as Jesus Christ gave His all for the church. You have a holy covenant, a promise that can never be broken, two lives blended into one.

The Old Code is only old in the sense that it was birthed a long time ago. When the Logos uttered, "Let there be light," truth had its genesis, and the Old Code springs from this fountain of truth. The Code is not old like a threadbare garment, ready to be cast away in favor of a new fashion. It will last forever. When Christ comes for His church, the reality of covenantal faithfulness will have its consummation. The bride and her bridegroom will meet face-to-face, and we will have eternity to enjoy our fellowship, because there will be no death "do us part."

May all of you find that love for your wives. May you learn to follow the Old Code of truth. You can be the image of Christ for your bride, living as a holy example of "God with us." And may you pass along these nearly forgotten treasures to hungry hearts who long for just a taste of the boundless life of holiness that God has provided in Christ.

The Unbroken Circle

Michael sat on the sofa and blew the dust off the old guitar case. He guessed that it must have been in the closet for more than ten years. He had seen it only once when he and Dad cleaned out an area to store some of Grandma's stuff when she died.

Inside the case he found a beautiful guitar, and he carefully pulled it out and placed it in his lap. The strings still seemed in good shape, and the tuning pegs still turned without complaining. Although he had no idea how to play it, he strummed it a few times just to hear how it sounded . . . Pretty bad! As he tried to tighten the strings to make it sound better, the front door opened. He turned to see his tired-looking father. "Hi Dad!"

His father looked at Michael and pulled off his coat. He smiled. "I see you found my guitar." He walked over and sat down next to his son. "Did you figure out how to tune it?"

Michael sighed and handed the guitar to his father. "Not really."

Michael's dad placed the guitar on his lap. "You know, I still play it sometimes when I'm alone. I even changed the strings about a year ago." With a few strums and tweaks of the pegs, the guitar began purring in perfect tones, and he gave it back to his son.

Michael plucked each string once and listened to the echo of the lowest note. He turned to his father and smiled. "You know, Dad, I was thinking. If you could teach me how to play, by the time summer comes I could be ready to go with you on your next trip. We could both go to Haiti and play for our mission church as a father and son duet." He handed the guitar back to his father. "So . . . would you teach me?"

Michael thought his father was going to cry, but the smile that broke out washed away any hint of sadness. His dad took the guitar and played a few chords, humming a bouncy version of "Amazing Grace." He finished with gusto, strumming rapid-fire and tapping his foot.

Michael laughed and clapped. "Dad, that was great!"

His dad let out a deep breath. "Well, it's been a while since I played that one. I'm a little rusty."

Michael looked at his dad's glowing face. He never seemed so happy before. "Well, maybe your playing's a little rusty, but your sword's not."

"My sword? What are you talking about?"

"Never mind. Can you play something else?"

"Sure. How about this one?"

As the sweet melody of "Will the Circle Be Unbroken?" drifted toward a back bedroom, Grandpa clutched a portrait of a pretty, gray-haired lady. "Maybe, Gladys, just maybe, I finally did something to mend our little circle. Forgive me for not being your knight in shining armor."

Benediction

The sun appears on the eastern horizon, its illuminating glow revealing the distant quest. Many enemy silhouettes appear, marching your way. They are massive. They seem unconquerable. Then a man mounted on a steed of silver dashes by. A woman is seated behind him, her arms firmly embracing his chest. With a strong, two-edged sword extended, his face set like flint, he charges toward the mounting army. With armor clanging, he pulls down his visor. He will plow into that seemingly impenetrable wall of marching soldiers. His lady, erect and unflinching, peers into the distance, her eyes set with wonder on the grand adventure. As they disappear toward the foreboding line, the man's armor reflects a gleaming ray into your eyes, and you sense his worth. He is a champion, a prince, a knight in shining armor.

You feel his joy. You feel your heart—the heart of a warrior, the inner longing to pursue an adventure, a quest for Almighty God.

Do you stand unprepared, without armor, sword, or shield? Do you feel naked, helpless, and unworthy to oppose the enemies of God? Look at your hands. Although no ropes or chains cross your flesh, do you feel bound just the same? Are you a slave of weakness, a prisoner of fear? Look at your

feet. There are no shackles, but do they feel rooted in clay—
the accepted, plastic manhood of the day?

"Come on home," your comrades call. "That knight
will soon perish, and then who will feed his children?"
Will you follow your friends? Will you return to the
comforts of mediocrity? Will they really give you solace as
they commiserate, as they beg you to be satisfied with cama-
raderie in the circles of the commonplace?

Living as a knight of the Old Code is not for the common man, nor for the squeamish. Nearly every day an army
to vanquish appears, and as we stare at those hulking shadows we realize our need for aid. God is our ever-present help
in time of need. He provides our armor, and so much more.
In every obstacle we face while on our quest for His kingdom, He will equip us for victory. As we charge into the fray,
relying completely on Him, we will topple every barrier. God
Himself will go into battle with us.

Yes, you must train. Physical endurance requires hard
work. Mental discipline demands diligent study. Spiritual
exercise must continue for as long as you draw breath. As
you wake up each day and grow closer to God, you will
know more fully the power of His resurrection and the fellowship of His sufferings. You will be conformed to the
image of Christ in your body day by day. While your muscles learn to swell with new energy, God will never allow
armies to rise up and overwhelm the sword and shield He
has placed in your hands.

Men, you already know the enemies on your horizons.
You've lived with them every day. I don't pretend to know
how hard your struggles are, but I can remind you of the
source of your help—Christ in you, the hope of glory.

You've seen the obstacles, now look at the provision.
Your armor, your sword, and your shield await your faithful

hand. The Spirit of God—the most powerful steed in the universe—will carry you to your quest. Your wife stands ready to be swept into the adventure God has set before you. This is her calling, to follow a man of God toward that dangerous horizon. With a little spit and polish, you can make your armor shine, and she'll recognize you as her warrior for righteousness.

Now get on your horse and ride! God will make you a champion!